mateur sports at all age levels are growing steadily in popularity. This growth has resulted in a corresponding need for people who know how to officiate along with the realization in the sports world of just how important officiating is to amateur competitive play. There's an old saying in sports that officiating can make or break a game. If the officials know what they're doing, the game is certainly safer and always more enjoyable for both players and spectators.

In outlining the duties of officials and the techniques used in top amateur and professional competition, *Calling the Play* lends a hand to all who feel that local play—be it playground game or regional league championship—deserves the best officiating possible. The book covers fifteen sports, each of which is treated in the following manner: officiating positions and their basic duties are described, along with the techniques and mechanics of officiating used at each position. In this way the reader feels that he or she is actually working at that position.

Among the sports covered:

- Baseball
- Football
- Basketball
- Tennis
- Soccer
- Track and field
- Swimming and diving
- Volleyball

Dolan also devotes attention to several popular sports that are not as widely played as those mentioned above. They are: boxing, ice hockey, softball, wrestling, lacrosse, badminton and water polo.

CALLING THE PLAY

*A Beginner's Guide to
Amateur Sports Officiating*

EDWARD F. DOLAN, JR.

ATHENEUM   1982   NEW YORK

LIBRARY OF CONGRESS CATALOGING IN PUBLICATION DATA

Dolan, Edward F., 1924–
  Calling the play.

  Bibliography: p.
  1. Sports officiating.   I. Title.
GV735.D64   796   81-66014
ISBN 0-689-11183-5   AACR2

FOR TOM AND VIRGINIA AYLESWORTH,
Good friends

ACKNOWLEDGMENTS

I AM INDEBTED to many fine people and organizations for their help in the preparation of this book.

First, for providing me with needed materials or answering specific questions, my thanks must go to the: Amateur Basketball Association of the USA, Amateur Hockey Association of the United States, American Youth Soccer Organization, Little League Baseball Inc., National Baseball Congress, National Collegiate Athletic Association, National Federation of State High School Associations, United States Badminton Association, United States Tennis Association, and United States Volleyball Association.

Many old and new friends answered my questions, gave suggestions, or checked sections of the manuscript for me. They were all gracious and generous with their time. And so my thanks go to: John Boccabella, Ralph Boccabella, Carl "Red" Brown, Nancy Dashcund of the United States Tennis Association, Michael Dolan, Wendy Gingell, Ray Schramm, Verle Sorgen, Inman Whipple, Milt Woods, and four very helpful and cooperative friends at American River College in Sacramento, California—Al Baeta, track and field and cross country coach; Ralph Freund, tennis coach; Bud Gardner of the Communications Department; and Ed Pegram, swimming and diving coach.

CONTENTS

x Contents

LIST OF ILLUSTRATIONS

CALLING THE PLAY

The World of Amateur Sports Officiating

IT'S A PARADOX: On the one hand, America's young people are accused of being lazy, overfed, and overweight, of never walking when they can ride, of never standing when they can sit. On the other, they're involved by the millions in athletics. They compete in just about every game that's played elsewhere in the world plus a few, such as football and baseball, that are distinctly our own. Further, the number of youngsters entering the sports picture seems to grow each year.

All this enthusiastic participation—along with that of the countless adults who now insist on being physically active for better health and a greater enjoyment of life—has done much to win the United States the reputation of being one of the most sports-conscious nations in the world.

But we're not here to talk about paradoxes. For the purposes of this book, what counts is that all the activity is presenting a challenging opportunity for thousands of Americans who, for reasons that can range from age to personal preference, wish to continue in or join a loved sport but not as a player. For them—and obviously for you because you're interested enough to open this book—the door to the world of amateur sports officiating is swinging wide.

It's a big and growing world. There was a time when organized competition, the kind that must have officials, was pretty much limited to our schools. But not today. You can find organized play everywhere. Baseball has its Little League, football its Pop Warner League. City recreation departments sponsor play in a wide variety of sports, among them tennis, softball, and soccer. Churches, service and social clubs, business groups, and even neighborhoods contribute teams to local leagues or maintain leagues of their own. And over the years the schools themselves have broadened their athletic programs; the traditional basketball, football, and baseball squads have been joined by such relative newcomers as volleyball, swimming, and soccer teams.

You can see the size of this world best, of course, by looking at the number of today's amateur officials. Unfortunately an exact total of all officials is impossible to come by. But three figures should give a good indication of just how great that total may be. Little League Baseball reports that it's served by approximately 84,000 volunteer umpires. The Amateur Hockey Association of the United States has over 7,400 registered officials on the books. The United States Tennis Association says that its list of certified umpires totals approximately 2,000. (Mind you, in the last two instances, the figures are for certified officials only.)

Though an exact total of all working officials can't be had, one thing can be said for certain. There are today more women active in officiating than ever before. The increasing popularity of such games as tennis, volleyball, and softball has in particular provided many fine openings for women. Commonly, city–sponsored soccer programs, especially those for younger players, are officiated by women. And the ranks of baseball and basketball officialdom are no longer exclusively male. In school basketball, the practice of using co-ed officiating teams is with us and is expected to continue blossoming in the coming years. As for baseball, Little League estimates that of its 84,000 volunteer umpires, some 15,000 are women. Of the USTA's certified umpires, about 25 percent are women.

Large and growing as it is, the world of officiating is in continual need of competent men and women. But the emphasis must be put on the word *competent*. Before you can hope to find a lasting place in officiating, you must meet the challenge of learning your trade. The challenge is a great and demanding one. There's more to the job than blowing a whistle, calling a few obvious plays, and keeping some young and exuberant competitors under appropriate control. There's much to be learned—from the most obscure rule interpretations to the most precise techniques for following and judging the action.

The purpose of this book is to assist you in your first days in the world of officiating. The whole idea is to help you build your confidence, your understanding of your job, and the excellence of your performance. To do this, we're going to look at more than a dozen sports in the next chapters and always put the emphasis on three points:

- The officials used and their varied responsibilities before, during, and after a game.
- The *mechanics of officiating.* This is the term for the many procedures and techniques that have been painstakingly developed over the years to enable an official to cover plays in the correct manner so that he is always where he's supposed to be and always able to see what he's supposed to see.
- The art of making those problem calls that can crop up at any time.

The hope is that this book will give you the feeling that you're actually in uniform and out there on the field, the court, or the mat.

Before we get to work, though, several points concerning the structure of the book need to be mentioned.

To begin, each chapter is devoted to an individual sport (the final chapter covers several less widely played games) and is as detailed as space will permit. But please don't look for a listing of the rules for each game. They're being omitted for three reasons.

First, rulebooks are readily available from your league or sponsoring organization and so there is no practical reason to include a listing here. Second, in their details the rules for a given sport sometimes vary from organization to organization or from age level to age level; a listing would need to take these variations into consideration and could easily prove confusing. Finally, again in their details, the rules have a habit of changing periodically; it's of no value to list a rule that by the time you read this book may well have been altered.

Certain general rules, however, will be mentioned. Their inclusion is necessary because of their direct application to an officiating technique under discussion. Unless otherwise specified, any rule that is mentioned applies to teen play.

As we go along, we'll talk about the scorekeeper needed in most of the games. His function and duties will be explained. But because he is ordinarily not an actual member of the officiating crew but an adjunct to it, the book won't go into his often complex system (especially in baseball and basketball) for keeping a running score and record of the game. Should you wish to try your hand at scorekeeping, you won't go wrong if you turn to two books to help you get started: *The World of Sports Statistics* by Arthur Friedman with Joel H. Cohen (Atheneum, 1978) and *Complete Handbook of Sports Scoring and Record Keeping* by Jack Richards and Danny Hill (Parker, 1974). Both cover all major sports.

Nor will there be mention of how to break into officiating. Each league or association has its own system and requirements for accepting officials. Your best bet here is to contact your league's local office or representative and then follow his advice. A friend who is already in officiating can also prove helpful in getting you started.

Finally, the writer is fully aware of the many women now working as amateur officials. Yet the generic pronoun *he* will be used throughout the coming pages. Please understand that this is not male chauvinism at work, but rather a desire for the word economy that comes of avoiding the sometimes unwieldy *he or she* and *him or her* constructions.

So welcome to the world of amateur sports officiating. Shall we begin?

1. Calling the Play

ON BECOMING a sports official, you assume two interrelated responsibilities. You commit yourself to seeing that your game or contest proceeds as it's meant to—that is, in accordance with its rules. At the same time you charge yourself with seeing that the action proceeds smoothly with as little interference on your part as possible.

There is a third commitment—the determination to set and maintain an atmosphere that best serves these responsibilities. While you must never bend the rules or neglect to enforce them, the needed atmosphere is not one of constant whistle blowing, a practice that unnerves the players by disturbing the rhythm of play and that can be avoided by a thorough understanding of what actually constitutes an infraction. Rather, the atmosphere must be one that makes the players themselves want to abide by the rules and prompts them to accept your decisions gracefully, if not altogether willingly.

In a nutshell, the atmosphere is one in which you are not the star. The players, as well they should be, are the center of attention while you remain in the background. As a friend who is a veteran football referee puts it, "If you're really good, you won't be noticed most of the time." But your influence, your quiet control of the game, will always be there and felt by the players.

Any official will tell you that it's a highly satisfying experience to meet these responsibilities. But he'll quickly add that there's nothing easy about his work. In their details the rules of any game are complex. The heat of competition can be fierce. The action can be amazingly fast and at times bewildering even to the most experienced eye. Yet an official is constantly required to make decisions that affect the tone and progress of play. They're to be solid decisions. And they're to be made in a fraction of a second.

Calling the Play—What it Takes

Every official must bring certain personal characteristics to the game if he is to enforce the rules properly and set the needed atmosphere. When listed, they tend to make him look something of a living saint, and the odds are that not one of us is favored with them all or even blessed with any to a full measure. Fortunately though, they're all characteristics that we can deliberately instill in ourselves. Further, with attention most can be developed to a high degree. Here's a look at them now.

Consistency You must call a game in the same manner from beginning to end. Possibly the single characteristic most appreciated by players and coaches, consistency requires that your actions and decisions remain the same in identical or similar circumstances.

A lack of consistency can't help but breed upset. Players simply don't know what to expect next if you vacillate in your decisions, perhaps ignoring an obvious foul at one point and then dealing with it severely at another. Confused, no one is able to play his best or his hardest; tempers fray and the enjoyment of the game is lost. On the other hand, if the players know that you can be depended on always to make your calls according to the same reasonable standards, they're able to relax and play smoothly within the confines you've set.

One of the greatest dangers to consistency is an official's tendency to even things up. Perhaps early on you make a poor call against Team A. Later hoping to square matters, you deliberately ignore another of Team A's infractions. At first glance it may seem the fair thing to do. It's anything but. Mistaken calls can be unintentionally made at any time, and you should never excuse yourself for them, but the effort to even things up only worsens matters because it mars the game with deliberately made poor calls. Your every decision should be based on the rules and their interpretations—and nothing else. If you come up with a poor call (and, being human, you will), your only course is to mark it in your mind and resolve never to repeat it.

Even worse is the attempt to even things up by shading your calls in favor of an obviously overmatched team. This is simply cheating, and it's going to be readily and angrily identified as such. Players, coaches, and spectators alike expect and want you to apply the rules in equal measure to both teams, and that is what you must do. The players on the weak team especially won't appreciate your compassion. They'll feel insulted.

In every game, certain rules are cut-and-dried (a player who crosses a sideline is out-of-bounds, and that's all there is to it), and they pose little or no threat to your consistency. But other rules are open to interpretation, and decisions on them require the use of your personal judgment (only certain body contacts in football, for instance, constitute pass interference). These are the calls that can cause trouble. The key to consistency is to apply the same interpretation to a judgmental rule throughout the game. The situations under which the interpretation is made will vary. But the basis for the interpretation will always remain the same—a fact that will be quickly noted and appreciated by everyone.

Integrity Your integrity—the impression of honesty that you convey—goes hand-in-hand with consistency. It's not only inconsistent but dishonest to shade your calls in favor of the weak team—or the home team—or the team quarterbacked by your nephew or coached by your closest friend.

The best safeguard for your integrity is always to live by that oldest of officiating rules: Call 'em as you see 'em. If you're working behind the plate in baseball, call each pitch a strike or a ball on the basis of the pitch itself and not on your feelings about the batter or the pitcher.

Your integrity must be protected at all times, both on and off the field. Never allow yourself to be put into a position where you can, justly or unjustly, be accused of dishonesty. Keep your personal opinions of the teams and the players to yourself. The same goes for your opinion (or private hope) as to which team will finally take the league championship. Think twice about working a game in which a relative or close friend is participating; some officials absolutely refuse to go near such a game. Above all, never bet—not even a nickel—on the outcome of any game you're to officiate.

Quick and Decisive You must be able to make your calls quickly and decisively. Do so and—assuming, of course, that your decision is a sound one—you'll much reduce the chances of an argument over any call.

Let's talk first about quickness. Your decision should come simultaneously with the action observed or as soon thereafter as possible. A hesitation may be needed to allow you to digest what you've seen, but it should be no more than just that—a hesitation. Too long a pause gives you a look of uncertainty; the door is immediately open to a challenge. Further, if you hesitate too long, you'll be forced to review in your mind what you've seen. You'd be surprised how hazy a recollection can become after just a few seconds. So go with your instincts and act swiftly.

Should you prove chronically hesitant, you'll likely fall into the trap of trying to compensate for your slowness. You'll start to anticipate the action. As you'll see later, anticipation is a most effective tool for making incorrect calls.

Any talk of quickness always brings up the matter of reaction time. Every official must have a fast reaction time—the ability to see, understand, and judge an action in an instant. In your first days as an official, your reaction time is likely to be a little slow, principally because of the extra time needed to identify what you're seeing and then to figure your judgment. Practice and experience will speed matters up.

But please be warned that your reaction time will be improved only to a certain degree. Each of us seems to have our own physiological limits in the speed of our reactions and reflexes. Once you reach your limit, you can really go no further, no matter how vigorously or religiously you may practice. If your reaction time is above average once you've gained officiating experience, you're in business. But if it continues to run slow and damages your work, then you should honestly face the fact that officiating isn't for you.

Even more than quickness, decisiveness will fend off arguments. Without being arrogant, you must always give the impression that you know what you're doing and what you've seen. Be timid or hesitant and you invite challenges; enough of them will come your way in the normal course of events—there's no need to add to the entertainment by asking for more. Decisiveness is especially important on controversial calls. A basic piece of officiating advice holds that while all calls should be clearly and definitely signaled, an extra shot of energy should be reserved for the close ones.

Attitude

Rapport You're not out to win a popularity contest but to call a solid game. But you're not out to make enemies, either. The game is between the two opposing sides, not between *you* and the sides. You need to establish a rapport with the players and the coaches—and even the spectators—that will encourage them to accept and cooperate with your way of doing things and your decisions. This is best done, of course, by putting into practice the characteristics that we've thus far discussed. Though not loving your every call, everyone will recognize your competence and fairness. Good rapport can't help but follow.

There are additional steps that you can take. First, even in the most difficult moments, always treat the players and coaches with courtesy and respect, and show by your demeanor that you want and expect them to reciprocate. One caution, however: Never let your courtesy and respect overflow into a look of chumminess that suggests favoritism or a desire to please. Your attitude should be friendly, yes, but tinged with an aloofness that leaves no one in doubt of your nonpartisan position. A proper distance maintained between you and the competitors will be of particular help when the time comes for a controversial call.

Second, though aloof, you should always be approachable, never cutting yourself off from the players or the coaches. Always be willing to hear complaints and questions. Answer both clearly and to the best of your ability. But again a caution: Don't allow the complaints or the questions to delay the game too long or interrupt it too often. Avoid long debates. Give your answer and restart the action as soon as possible. The teams are there to play, not to bicker with you. Incidentally, there's nothing like restarting the action to get you safely past the uproar over a disputed call.

Finally, enjoy your work. By your attitude, let the players and coaches see that you like what you're doing and are enjoying the game. And don't leave your sense of humor at home. Let it show at the right moments.

Poised and Calm   The action is going to be fast. The players are going to be on the move. There are going to be moments of confusion and moments of high, sometimes almost unbearable, tension. There are going to be times when the players are furious over your decisions or the fans decide that you've achieved the status of a blind idiot.

It almost goes without saying that no matter what happens, you must remain poised and in control of your emotions. When you lose your head, your vision and judgment immediately blur—and a poor call is almost certain to follow. When you fly into a rage with a player who challenges a call, you lose his respect and a degree of your control over the game. When you become visibly addled or upset by the action, your uncertainty spreads to the players and may damage their performance and timing; miscues and a harvest of infractions can be expected.

While you must remain in control of yourself at all times, your poise and calm are particularly needed in moments of high tension. These are the moments with the greatest potential for fouls, injuries, and violent outbursts. While you cannot be expected to exercise full control over the emotions of the players, you must conduct yourself in a way that doesn't worsen matters and that encourages the players to keep their heads. A poised and calm show of your authority, communicating that you're on top of things, is a must for bringing the game through a moment of crisis and returning it to normal. In a word, it's called leadership.

If you let them get away with it, the unhappy reactions of the players and the spectators to your decisions can really damage your self-control. Each call, as has been said before, must be made on the basis of the rules and their interpretations, and not on some expected reaction to it. Should you let go of yourself and begin to think about reactions, you'll find yourself nervously trying to make the easy or popular call rather than the right one. At that moment, your value as an official ends.

All this is not to say that you shouldn't actually feel excited or upset.

You're neither an automaton nor a marble statue. What counts is not that you feel turmoil, but that you keep it to yourself, under control, and never let it jeopardize your work or upset the players. It takes practiced self-discipline. It's a self-discipline that every top official has.

Dedication You may think it a somewhat fancy term—this word *dedication*—but you can't do without it. Solid officiating requires that you stay on top of things from start to finish. In its turn, staying on top requires a complex of attributes—everything from enthusiasm, attention to the action, and cooperation with your fellow officials to an intense physical and mental effort. It's exhausting to keep these attributes continually and effectively in play—and impossible to do so without dedication to your job and your sport.

Dedication is easily translated as "hustle," that most respected of characteristics in an athlete. Though tiring, constant hustle will actually reduce the strain of your work. For one thing, admiring it as they do, the players and coaches will like you for it and will then more quickly respond to your influence. For another, since you're obviously not asleep out there, they'll be more inclined to trust and accept your decisions. And for still another, you'll increase your own enjoyment by being thoroughly involved in the game and by knowing that you're giving your best.

Hustle begins the moment the game or contest begins. Never try to accustom yourself to the action by easing into it. Get on top of it right away; otherwise you'll give a poor first impression that may be difficult to overcome. And stay on top until the game is over, completely over. No letting down along the way, especially in the final minutes when the brains and legs are tiring fast.

Something now has to be said about the physical demands of hustle. Some sports, among them tennis and track, put little physical strain on the official; mental strain is, of course, quite another matter. But most sports are physically tough on the officiating crew and some—football, basketball, and soccer are prime examples—can be classed as downright rugged. It's been estimated, for instance, that a basketball official easily covers between two and three miles in a game. A soccer referee can log as many as six.

The point here, obviously, is that you must be up to the physical demands of the job. You'll damage the game, not to mention yourself, if you can't get all the way through in reasonable comfort. Whether you're a newcomer or an oldtimer, you should condition yourself before the start of the season. Follow a simple, gradual conditioning program that puts the accent on activities and exercises that develop endurance; watch your diet; get ample rest. The conditioning program will not only build your stamina but will also help to protect you against such classic early season injuries as torn muscles. You should also make an appointment with your doctor for a checkup.

Calling the Play—The Basics

Just as you must bring certain personal characteristics to officiating, so must you also bring along a set of basic commitments. Regardless of what your sport may be, they'll be needed. You must first:

Know the Rules Though it can be helpful, it's not necessary to have played the game that you're to officiate. But you must know the game itself and its rules—from one end to the other. Otherwise (need it be said?) you're going to be lost out there.

But you need to know more than just the rules themselves. You should also understand the reasons for the rules, how rules are related to each other, and how certain of them are to be interpreted. Then you'll have a thorough grasp of the game that will enable you to make your decisions quickly, confidently, and most importantly of all, correctly.

Special attention must be given to rule interpretation. Unless looked upon in a certain way, it can cause you trouble.

As was said earlier, some rules are cut-and-dried and can be interpreted literally. Others are loosely worded, deliberately so, to enable them to embrace a wide variety of possible situations. (The pass interference rule in football is a case in point.) Enforcement in these cases becomes a matter of your interpretation of the rule involved. Here you're up against that most difficult of decisions—the judgment call. Faced with it, you can get yourself into difficulty in two ways.

If you interpret the rules too literally, you risk being whistle happy, stopping the action on every borderline incident and ruining the game for spectators and players alike. If you interpret the rules too loosely, you chance letting punishable fouls slip past; if the wrong ones get past, the game can become too one-sided and even dangerous for the players. Your job is to go down the middle, on the one hand not being too much of a stickler, and on the other not being too lenient. It's a difficult path to walk, especially in your first days of officiating.

Fortunately, you're not left alone when it comes to rule interpretation. Every sport's governing body has issued interpretations of the rules, plus examples of plays that serve as illustrations. These interpretations should be studied closely, learned thoroughly, and kept in mind at all times. You can further help yourself especially on borderline calls, by remembering what Oswald Tower, a member of the Basketball Rules Committee for an illustrious half century, once said. He held that *the essential purpose of the rules is to penalize a player whose illegal act, whether unintentional or deliberate, places his opponent at a disadvantage.*

In practical terms what his view boils down to is this: When you see some action that can be classed as an infraction if you interpret the applicable rule literally, forget it if it poses no disadvantage to the opposing player, places him in no danger, or impedes the game in no way. Look on it as an incidental occurrence of no consequence and let the game proceed. It's a sensible and helpful approach because it enables you to see an infraction in its true proportions. The minor, passing ones quickly separate themselves from the more serious ones.

Your study of the rules shouldn't be limited to the rule book itself. Talk them over with your friends and fellow officials. Attend the classes, seminars, and workshops held by your league or sports association for its officials; they're great not only for explaining and clarifying the rules, but for keeping you abreast of changes and expanding interpretations. If there's not one already in town, you might form a study group for discussions. And be sure to follow the procedure used by many top officials: Review the rule book in its entirety on the night before a game and then in the morning, double-check those rules and playing situations that have given you particular difficulty in the past.

Cooperate with Your Fellow Officials "If you're working a sport that requires more than one official, the officiating itself becomes a team sport. All the cooperation that makes a team click has to go into it."

Speaking is a friend who is a longtime amateur baseball umpire. He's right. Just as a team can't hope to win unless the players work together, neither can an officiating crew call a good game unless all the members pull in the same direction. Without teamwork, calls are going to be missed. Without teamwork, there's going to be a tension that spreads quickly to the players.

You already know why you must be consistent in your decisions as an individual. For the same reasons consistency is needed by the crew—and it takes teamwork to achieve it. All the crew members should try to interpret the rules in the same way. All should try to regard infractions in the same light with no one man being substantially more or less severe than his companions. The result will be an afternoon of decisions that are as uniform as possible. There are bound to be some differences in the calls, individuals being what they are, but an effort must be made to keep the variations slight. If the officials all work together for a mutual consistency, the game will proceed smoothly with whistles sounding only when they're necessary. If one man is too much out of step with the others, the officiating is going to be uneven.

The degree of teamwork among officials varies from sport to sport. In some games you're assigned specific duties and are expected to confine yourself to them. If you're a tennis linesman, for instance, you're to call "outs" and "faults" in your own area and no other; here, intrusion on a fellow official's responsibilities is considered to be just that—an intrusion; for you, teamwork means limiting yourself to your specific duties and giving outside assistance on request only. Other sports, however, give you a greater freedom, and in the name of teamwork you must exercise it. In football you begin each play with a set of primary duties. Once you've performed them, you must lend your fellow officials a hand with theirs. Should you do less—relax and drop out of the action—the crew will no longer have the play completely surrounded. Some vital call may be missed.

In sports such as football teamwork calls for each official to render a decision whenever he's in the position to do so, regardless of whether the action at hand is inside or outside the area of his immediate responsibility. Unless the game rules or your league's manual of officiating give specific jurisdiction to a certain official, you should always be ready to make decisions on any play or infraction that you see. Ideally, any play should be called by the man with the best view of it.

Teamwork requires that certain personality traits be left at home. Topping the list is any tendency to feed your sense of superiority by doubting the abilities of your fellow officials; you simply can't concentrate on your own job if you're constantly wondering if they can do theirs; a trust in their capabilities will usually be well placed. Next comes any tendency to dominate the crew; even if you're the head man, never throw your weight around or try to be the star of the game; otherwise you can count on some lost cooperation. Finally, there's the tendency to be over-sensitive about your prerogatives; don't become upset if a fellow official makes a call that he's entitled to make but which you feel was more rightfully yours; be happy for his help and remember that he may have been better positioned than you for the call.

Above all, teamwork requires that you never openly challenge a fellow official's decision, even though you may violently disagree with it or know without doubt that he's wrong. Nor should you ever show the teams that you think he's made a mistake. And never argue with him in an attempt to have him change the call. There will be times when he asks for your advice and assistance. By all means, give it if you're in a position to do so. But save all unsolicited suggestions and comments for the crew conferences at intermission time or after the game, or wait until the two of you are in your car and on your way home. *Nothing must be done on the field to suggest to the players that there is divisiveness on the crew.* A solid front is a must for a well-called and well-controlled game.

Calling the Action You must call 'em as you see 'em, the old axiom goes. But you must see them correctly before you can call them. Incorrect calls can put a team at a terrible disadvantage and even alter the outcome of the game. It's no easy task to call plays and infractions correctly, especially the close ones. Constant vigilance is required. And constant attention must be given to the following four pointers:

- *Observe every play at close quarters.* In most sports (we'll point out the few exceptions in the coming chapters), the best view of any action can be had from a few feet away. Up close you're able to see the action in full and judge whether any movement or maneuver actually constitutes an infraction. You're also better able to judge the results of the play— the exact yardage gained in football, the runner safe or out in baseball.
- *Never guess at a decision.* An infraction must be clearly and unmistakably seen before it can be called. If your view of a suspected foul is at

all blocked, forget the decision or leave it to someone else. You may have missed a critical detail that turns the seeming foul into a legal action.

• *Don't call an infraction unless you see it in its entirety, right from the beginning.* When picked up near their end or midway through, some actions seem to be fouls when actually they're not. Let's say that a tackler in football, on being blocked from the front, turns with the force of the impact and goes down with his back to the blocker. If you catch the action late, you can be fooled into thinking you're seeing a clip. But there's no clip unless the initial contact is from the rear.

• *Never anticipate a call.* See the action through to its finish; stay with it until it's completely over; then make the call. When you act too soon, you risk missing some final split-second circumstance that can negate your decision. Imagine you're a baseball umpire working at first when a double-play ball is hit. The force is made at second. The ball comes whipping into first well ahead of the runner. Certain of the play's outcome, you swing away with the "out" signal just as the ball hits the baseman's glove. But then he drops or bobbles the thing. The runner is safe and you're left looking foolish. While always wanting to make your calls quickly and decisively, at exactly the right moment, you're better off being an instant too late than an instant too early.

Protect the Players Though some sports are far less hazardous than others, there isn't an athletic competition to be found that doesn't pose some physical danger for the participants. Injuries are a constant threat. They're sure to occur from time to time. But good officiating can help reduce them to a minimum.

You must never let yourself forget the welfare of the players. Anyone guilty of unduly rough play or unsportsmanlike conduct should be immediately penalized and warned that continued misconduct will get him disqualified. Then without speaking directly to him let your subsequent actions and attitudes encourage him to play properly. If he persists in his misbehavior, you shouldn't hesitate to dismiss him.

If you put to work the officiating qualities that were discussed early in this chapter, you'll find that they'll do much to encourage injury-free play. Your alertness and the consistency of your calls, for instance, will quell any urge to sneak infractions past you. Your ability to be on top of a play and to whistle the ball dead at the right moment will prevent much of the last-second scrambling and battling—so commonly seen in football—that can easily result in injury. Your poise and calmness will help keep tempers under control in moments of especially high tension.

In working for the welfare of the players, you'll be doing far more than protecting them against injury. You'll be making your contribution to that most basic aim in sports—to promote a sense of competitiveness that, though vigorous, is always fair, self-controlled, and aboveboard.

Know the Mechanics of Officiating The mechanics of officiating are the procedures that officials follow in administering a game. Varying from sport to sport—but markedly similar in many respects—they cover the duties of each official before, during, and even after the game. In particular, they outline the techniques that each should use to insure that he's able to cover every play fully.

These techniques have been painstakingly developed through years of experience. You should find most of them easy to remember because they're based on practicality and logic But remembering is one thing; mastery is quite another. Mastery requires hard work both on and off the field.

On the field, never let your mind stray from what you're doing; note your mistakes with an eye to correcting them and your ways of doing things with an eye to improving them. Off the field, review what you did right and especially what you did wrong—and why. Don't be afraid to ask for pointers from your fellow officials. Never be in such a hurry to get home that you miss the postgame critique session that most officiating crews traditionally hold. Attend as many workshops and clinics for officials as you can find. (Incidentally, no matter how experienced you become, never give up attending them; they're excellent technique refreshers.) And whenever viewing a game that's being officiated by a master, study him closely and learn from him.

The results of your work will be worth the effort. Once you master the techniques of officiating, you'll begin to feel the cool confidence that comes with knowing where you're supposed to be at all times, what you're looking for there, and exactly what you're supposed to do. At that time, you can bet that someone will begin studying you.

2. Baseball

DEPENDING ON THE LEVEL of play, our national pastime is handled by one to six field officials, plus an official scorekeeper. Professional games use four men during the regular season and jump to six for All-Star and World Series play. Most amateur games, however—sometimes because there aren't enough officials at hand and sometimes because a school or league budget can't handle a full crew—are worked by just two officials. In this chapter, we'll concentrate on the two-official system, adding a section on what to do should you ever be called on to work a one-umpire game.

The Officials

The officials used on a two-man crew are the *plate umpire* and the *field umpire.* To see their duties, let's put you to work at each spot.

The Plate Umpire Regardless of the number of men on the crew, you're the senior official and are designated in the rules as the umpire-in-chief.

Your station is behind the catcher and your primary duties there are three. You (1) call and keep track of the balls and strikes registered on the batter, (2) signal whether balls are batted fair or foul, and (3) render all decisions on the batter and on runners coming into the plate.

In a two-official game, you'll also be called upon to make decisions at third base when the field umpire is busy elsewhere. More later of how this works.

Though these are your primary jobs, your work doesn't stop with them. The rules give you a string of other responsibilities. You're to:

- Inspect the field and playing equipment before (and, if necessary, during) the game, always with an eye to safety.
- Receive the batting orders from the teams before play begins, announce the ground rules under which the game is to be played, formulate any ground rules on which the teams can't agree, and appoint an official scorekeeper.
- Call and signal "play ball" when the game is to begin.
- Call "time" when the ball is dead and play is to stop, and "play ball" when the action is to resume.
- Announce each batter and substitute.
- See to it that the players take their gloves and other loose equipment to the bench when leaving the field.
- Assess penalties for such infractions as balks, interference, delays in the game, unsportsmanlike conduct, and unwarranted disputes over umpire calls.
- Disqualify players, send coaches from the field, or clear the benches if necessary.

You must also keep track of charged conferences. Without being penalized, the team on defense may usually confer on strategy and the like three times during a seven-inning game, and once per frame in extra innings. The team on offense is usually permitted one conference per inning.

As umpire-in-chief, you're the ultimate authority in a number of matters. You're the official who:

- Makes the final decisions on all questions not covered by the rules.
- Calls an end to the game if conditions become unfit for play.

1.

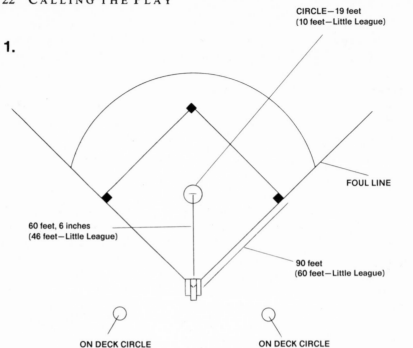

CIRCLE—19 feet
(10 feet—Little League)

FOUL LINE

60 feet, 6 inches
(46 feet—Little League)

90 feet
(60 feet—Little League)

ON DECK CIRCLE   ON DECK CIRCLE

- Forfeits a game for prescribed infractions by players, coaches, or spectators.
- Reports any team protest to the league or sponsoring organization.

Finally, depending on the policies of your league, you may be given a final charge. You may be instructed not to permit any player who has been knocked unconscious to resume play that day without a written authorization from a doctor.

The Field Umpire Your job is to call the plays at the bases, declaring runners out or safe. In a two-official game, you should work all three bases whenever possible. As mentioned above, there will be times when you'll be unable to take care of third base and the plate umpire will cover for you there.

* * *

In your capacity as a field umpire, you may call time and such infractions as balks, illegal pitches, and defacement of the ball by the pitcher. You may also eject any player or coach from the game for unsportsmanlike conduct and other flagrant violations.

You'll often hear yourself referred to as a base umpire. To keep the record straight, *field umpire* is the term used when there is just one official on the bases. When more than one man is used, the term becomes *base umpire*. Each official is then given a base to cover and is required to make the appropriate calls there.

The Official Scorekeeper Amateur games may or may not have an official scorekeeper; it all depends on the level of play. Though the scorekeeper is not actually a member of the umpiring crew, a word about him must be said here to make the record complete. His job is not only to keep an accurate record of the score but also to maintain a running record of the game. The scorekeeper will usually be in touch with the crew only when there are changes in the lineup or when questions arise over such matters as the number of outs, the scoring of a run, or the problem of hit-versus-sacrifice.

The job of score- and recordkeeping is one of the most demanding and complex in this game that loves its statistics. The scorer must be meticulous and conscientious; needless to say, a love for statistics is more than a little help. In professional and top amateur play, the job often goes to a sportswriter. In all circumstances, it should be entrusted only to someone who understands and is deeply interested in baseball.

The Mechanics of Umpiring

As you know, the mechanics of officiating are those carefully developed procedures and techniques that enable you best to cover a play and see what you're supposed to see. In baseball, they're known as the *mechanics of umpiring*. If you learn and then follow them at all times, you'll be assured of calling a good game, a game that is fair to both teams. First, let's go behind the plate.

The Plate Umpire at Work As soon as you move behind the plate, you must take a position that will enable you to call balls and strikes. Two positions may be used. You may either crouch down and look over the catcher's shoulder or settle in so that you're sighting in just above his head.

Both systems have their advantages and, unless your league specifically rules that one or the other must be used, it will be up to you to decide which you'll choose. Your choice, of course, will go to the one that proves more comfortable and thus enables you to do your best work. In the over-the-shoulder crouch, you'll have a very clear view of the strike zone (the area over any part of the plate between the batter's armpits and knees when he assumes a natural batting stance), and you'll be able to take a particularly close look at pitches low and inside. The over-the-head position permits you to move easily with the pitches and gives you a better view of throws that arrive high and outside.

The over-the-shoulder style is recommended for beginners, and so we'll put the emphasis on it.

The crouch here is over the catcher's inside shoulder—that is, the shoulder that is closer to the batter. If the batter is right-handed, settle down behind the catcher's left shoulder. If the batter is a lefty, switch to the opposite shoulder. Crouch well down and make certain that you have a clear view out to the mound.

Now the fun begins. In the course of an ordinary seven-inning game, you're going to see and judge well over 100 deliveries (when Don Larsen posted his perfect World Series game in 1956, he threw a minimum number of pitches, yet they managed to total out at ninety-seven). When a batter swings and misses, there's no problem. But when he lets the pitches go by, some—if not most—of them are going to give you trouble.

Near the top of the troublemakers' list are inside pitches—deliveries that bring the ball in on the batter's side of the plate. When they're well inside, they may cause him to pull back or jump away, leaving you with the impression that they actually didn't cross some part of the plate but were outside its boundaries. The best way to avoid a bad call here is to watch the ball and not the batter. In fact, *on all pitches, watch the ball and not the batter or the catcher.* Its location as it comes in over the plate is all that counts.

Also—here and on all pitches—keep your eyes open every minute of the time. There's always a tendency to blink when the batter swings, when the ball thumps into the catcher's mitt, or when, as it's flying towards you, the ball seems about to hit your face. Blinks are natural, but they have to be overcome. They can cause you to lose track of the spot where the ball passes over the plate.

Low balls are also difficult to judge. For your best view, get down as low as you can. Again, watch the ball. No matter what the batter does, keep your mind on where the ball is in relation to his knees at the time it crosses the plate. If it's at or above the knees and over the plate, it's a strike.

Curve balls pose a problem because they so often end up in the catcher's mitt below or to one side or the other of the strike zone. Once again, eyes on the ball. Is it in the strike zone at the time it passes the plate? If so, it's a strike. Where it then meets the catcher's glove is of no consequence.

If you're not careful, a wily catcher can hand you as much trouble as the pitches. Often he'll shift his body or move his glove in an effort to reposition the ball. Don't be fooled. Watch the ball and ignore the histrionics. Many umpires feel you should automatically assume that a questionable pitch is a ball if the catcher attempts some action meant to alter the flight path in your eyes.

All strikes must be signaled as such. This is done by swinging your arm out and downward in a chopping motion (see the section on signals). In the same instant, you must call "strike." The chopping action should be deliberate and should be done in a somewhat exaggerated fashion so that the signal can be easily seen and understood by both spectators and distant players. The call should be loud and clear. You may signal a strike while facing the plate, or you may turn sideways to the plate.

No signal is given for a ball. Your lack of action says it all. But you must call "ball."

It's not necessary or customary to call the strikes and balls by number —strike one or ball one. "Strike" or "ball" will do. You must, however, keep an accurate count on the batter. The count should be communicated to the field whenever you think wise or whenever there seems to be some doubt about it. To signal the count, hold up both hands, displaying the number of strikes with the fingers of the right hand and the number of balls with the left hand. When three fingers must be shown, tradition calls for the middle, ring, and little fingers to be extended. A closed fist indicates there are either no balls or no strikes. Two closed fists mean a full count.

The count should be called aloud as it is being shown. Always call the number of balls first. Again, there's no need to call, "two balls and one strike." "Two and one," is all that's expected. Make the call in a strong voice and hold your upraised hands steadily so that you're clearly heard and seen. The count is best shown during the gap in the action after the ball has been returned to the mound and before the pitcher is ready for his next delivery.

You're bound to get into hot water sooner or later if you depend on your memory alone for the count, and so you should carry a counter at all times. Held in one hand, it enables you to click the number of balls and strikes into little windows in its face. You'll be able to order one through any sports shop. As a beginner, you should spend some time practicing with the counter and growing accustomed to its use so that in the heat of your first games you won't forget it's there.

As the plate umpire, you're in the best position to judge whether balls hit along the first and third baselines are fair or foul; in a two-umpire game, you're the only official able to see along the third baseline. As soon as the batter connects, you should step away from the plate and sight along the appropriate baseline. If the ball is hit at or beyond first, the field umpire will also sight along the line.

Two simple signals are used on baseline hits. If the ball is foul, bring your arm up horizontally, point to foul territory, and call "foul." Point to fair territory for fair balls; it is not necessary, however, to call "fair." Both signals should be executed purposefully and should be held for a moment so that they're clearly seen.

The Field Umpire at Work Whenever a batter comes to the plate, you'll need to position yourself according to the number of runners on base. Using illustration 2, let's look at your various starting positions and then the moves that must follow when the ball is hit.

At the start of a half-inning or at any time when the bases are empty, station yourself a comfortable distance beyond first base (Point A). Umpires have individual preferences concerning distance, and you'll undoubtedly settle on yours in time, but for a start try a spot about ten feet off the bag. Position yourself slightly in foul territory.

2.

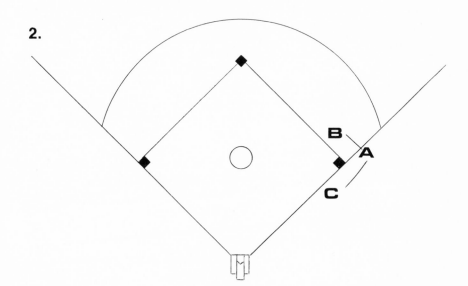

Once the ball is hit, you must shift to a position that will give you a clear view of the action to come at first. You must be able to see the baseman's glove when the ball is thrown to him after being fielded. You must be able to see his feet in relation to the bag. And you must be able to see the runner's feet as he crosses the bag.

When the ball travels to the batter's left or is fielded inside the baselines, your best bet is to move into fair territory behind the first-second baseline (Point B). Here you'll have the needed clear view of first base. And quite as important, you'll be safely away from any accidental entanglement with the action. For one thing, no matter from what part of the diamond the fielded ball is thrown, you'll be well clear of its line of flight.

For a ball that is hit to the batter's right or beyond the infield, move to a spot in foul territory several feet to the homeside of first (Point C). Your view of the bag and the action there will be unobstructed. And again, you'll be out of the path of the thrown ball.

Once a runner is on first, you'll need to shift your position for the next batter. Some officials recommend that you station yourself about midway between the mound and second base (Point A), shading slightly to the

3.

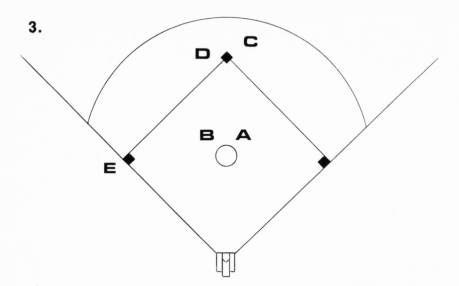

first base side of the pitcher. When you take the position, be sure to check that you're not obstructing any fielder's view of the plate. The position enables you to cover plays at any base.

You may continue to hold this position if there are runners at first and second. Or you can switch to the third base side of the pitcher (Point B). You should still remain about halfway between the mound and second base. This position may also be taken when a runner is at second or third, when there are runners at second and third, or when the bases are loaded.

Little League recommends a series of slightly different positions. Point C is used when the runner is on first base. There is a move to Point D when he advances to second or when there are men at first and second. Point E is the position when a runner is at third, when there are runners at second and third, when the runners are at first and third, or when the bases are full. When you take any of the positions shown in the illustration, be sure that you locate yourself so that you have a clear view of the bases being covered and of the plate.

On seeing a ball hit, follow its line of travel to the defender who fields it. Then track the ball to the base to which it is thrown, at the same time stepping towards that base so you'll be in a position for the play there. Do not—*repeat, do not*—decide on your own that a play is to be made at a given base. Hesitate until you're absolutely certain. A premature decision can head you for a base only to have the ball go elsewhere at the last moment.

You must, of course, always be ready to cover all the bases. At times when he is not otherwise occupied, the plate umpire will give you an assist by covering third. For instance, let's say there are runners at first and second. The batter sends a high hopper over the shortstop. The plate umpire should immediately move up the foul side of the third baseline to a point where he can cover the runner arriving from second. He should be ready to head back to the plate in the event that the runner is able to start for home. For your part, you'll need to cover the runner coming into second and then the batter heading for first.

Every runner coming into a base (or into home plate) must be judged safe or out on arrival. Two actions are used to signal the decision. If you see that the runner is out, you should throw your arm above your head with your fist clenched and your thumb upthrust; simultaneously call "out." Should the runner be safe, crouch down with outstretched arms and your palms turned downward. Your arms may be held out to the front or the sides. Often you'll see umpires execute a scissoring action with their arms. Be sure to call "safe."

There are two cardinal rules for covering a play at any base. First, without acting prematurely get into position for the call as quickly as possible so you're physically and mentally set to make the decision. If you become involved in a race with the runner, your vision will likely be blurred and your mind too rushed for a competent call.

Second, stay with the play from its beginning to end. Don't turn away until you've seen everything. Otherwise you may miss an action vital to your decision. A sliding runner, for instance, may first appear safe only to miss the bag and be tagged out. Or a baseman who seems certain to make a tag may drop the ball.

The problem of covering plays at two bases can be a real headache. All that can be said is that you must get to the base where the first of the calls is to be made. Immediately on making your decision there, turn to the second play. You'll likely find this job especially difficult when you're first umpiring, but matters should ease as you gain experience. Just be sure of one thing: in the excitement of making the first call, don't forget that you've got another play on your hands.

Umpires over the years have developed a special technique for calls at first base. Let's say that a ball is hit when the bases are empty. Move from your starting position to your coverage spot. Now watch the defender who fields the ball. Then watch the ball as it is thrown to the base. In the instant before its arrival, switch to the baseman's foot to be sure he's touching the bag. Now depend on your ears. Which sound do you hear first—the ball hitting the glove or the runner's foot touching the base? The answer will give you your decision. Stay with the action all the while, making sure that the baseman's foot remains in contact with the bag and that he doesn't drop the ball.

At times the thrown ball is going to be in the dirt, with the baseman forced to scoop it up. Before making your decision, you'll need a brief moment—no more than a hesitation—to check yourself on what you've seen.

On Your Own

If you stay in amateur officiating long enough, you're going to umpire a game by yourself one day. Sooner or later some colleague will be ill or out of town (or just plain won't show up), and no replacement will be available. Or you may find yourself in a lower classified league that can afford only one umpire per game. So what to do?

You're sure to run into divided opinion on the question of where to position yourself in a one-umpire game. Some officials say that you should work behind the pitcher at all times, and others advise that you divide your time between the plate and the mound. Each system has its advantages and disadvantages. It will be up to you to decide which you find more valuable and comfortable. One point, however, must always be kept in mind: For safety's sake, always work behind the pitcher if you're without any protective equipment.

The officials who favor the behind-the-pitcher system agree that you may sacrifice some accuracy in your calls of balls and strikes, and fair and foul hits—but say that you'll even things up by your coverage of the bases and by the consistency produced by handling the game from a single location. The plate-and-mound supporters feel that your toughest decisions will usually be made at the plate, so you should be stationed there for as much of the game as possible. There you're in the best shape to judge critical strikes and balls, fair and foul hits, and close scoring plays. Under certain circumstances you'll shift to the mound and give the base coverage a fair shake. It's been estimated that the single umpire spends from two-thirds to three-quarters of his time at the plate.

Most umpires seem to prefer the plate-and-mound system. They recommend that you station yourself behind the plate when (1) the bases are empty or full, (2) there is a runner at third only, and (3) there are runners at second and third.

When you need to switch positions, you should take your place just off and behind the mound. If the pitcher is a right-hander, you'll give yourself a better view of the plate by sighting past his right arm. Move to the left arm for a southpaw. In each position, be sure to stay out of the background for the hitter so that you don't distract him. It's advised that you work behind the mound when (1) there is a runner at first or second, (2) there are runners at first and second, and (3) there are runners at first and third.

On being faced with a one-umpire game, you may receive an offer of help from an inexperienced someone in the stands. Should you accept? Most umpires feel that a game is better off without an untrained assistant, and say that volunteers should be politely turned down unless both team managers want the extra hand. If you are forced to use volunteer help, be sure to get him into the proper starting position for each batter, and then if necessary, give him a few helpful suggestions between innings. Take care, though, not to confuse him with a welter of instructions.

Problem Calls

Every game is going to bring its share of problem calls. To help you handle them, here is a list of the umpire's most common headaches, along with some suggestions for their care and treatment. We'll start at the plate.

Check Swings A swing and a miss, of course, is a strike. But a batter is permitted to "check his swing" at any time—that is, hold back when he sees a pitch not to his liking. You'll need to call a ball if he successfully checks and the pitch is a bad one, and a strike if it's a good one. If he fails to check successfully, the swing is to be considered a full one, with the call then being a strike no matter where the pitch ends up.

There was a time when fans thought the batter had to bring the bat out over the plate and "break" his wrists for a swing to be full. Actually, the swing is full when the bat is carried to a point over the center of the plate, with the "breaking" of the wrists having nothing to do with the matter. If the batter manages to hold back before reaching the middle of the plate, he's checked. If not, his swing is full.

Check swings are hard to call because you have to watch two little dramas at once—the flight of the ball and the check itself. In time, experience will help your decisions, but no matter how long you're in officiating the check is going to give you trouble. Your best bet here, as on any problem call, is never to forget that the check can happen at any moment and to be constantly on the lookout for it.

Whenever you're in doubt about a check swing, don't hesitate to turn to the field umpire for assistance. His view of the swing is often better than yours. Step out from the plate and indicate that you need help. He'll signal a strike by clenching his right hand or nodding. A shake of the head means a ball.

Ball in the Dirt   The batter nicks the ball on its topside. It's driven almost straight down. It strikes the plate or the ground just behind or the batter's box. Then it heads into fair territory and settles there. What's the call?

The hit is fair if the ball misses the batter while he's in the box or if the catcher doesn't get his hands on it while it's in foul territory. If the ball hits the batter in the box or the catcher while he's in foul territory, then it's a foul.

The decision is simple enough. But with the action unfolding so quickly, the problem of seeing the ball touch either player can be anything but simple. And with both men moving, your vision may be momentarily screened—usually at exactly the wrong moment. Your safeguard here is the usual one: be alert and ready for the play at all times. Sometimes the field umpire may be able to help you. Many umpires think it wise to call the ball foul whenever there's any doubt about the decision; all things considered, it may be the fairest decision that can be made.

Hit Batters A batter is allowed to take first base when hit by a pitched ball. If he's obviously hit, the call is a cinch. But some hits are anything but obvious.

Remember Game Five of the 1969 World Series, when Lou DiMuro was working the plate? A pitch hit the dirt at the feet of the Mets' Cleon Jones. Jones headed for first base, only to be called back. He claimed he had been hit on the foot. DiMuro disagreed. The argument raged until the umpire took a look at the ball. It was smudged with black shoe polish. Jones got his base.

There will be times when you'll be in the same position as DiMuro. A pitch will graze a batter's uniform so slightly that there won't be a visible ripple of cloth or the slightest deflection of the ball. Or the ball will land in the dirt and be obscured by an explosion of dust. Or the batter, turning or dodging, will screen the contact from your view. Or you'll be faced with an actor who, though untouched, manages an Academy Award performance of pain and insult. In all these instances, you hold but one option: the batter must not be awarded first base unless you actually see the ball hit him, or unless, as in the Jones incident, there is some other proof of the contact. The field umpire may be able to help with the decision at times.

The batter, incidentally, must make an effort to avoid the ball before he can be sent to first. Ignore the call if you think that he made no effort to get out of the way and deliberately allowed himself to be hit.

You're also not to send him to first should he swing at the pitch and then be hit.

Interference and Obstruction Though baseball is not a contact sport, there are a number of occasions when the players touch each other. Some body contacts are legal, chief among them, of course, the baseman's tag and the runner-catcher collisions at home plate on close scoring plays. Others are illegal because they give one team an unfair advantage over the other. Whether they're unintentionally or deliberately committed, you must call them.

Illegal contacts fall into two categories: *interference and obstruction.* For the purposes of definition, interference refers to any act that hinders a batter, a fielder, or the catcher and keeps him from doing his job. For instance, you're to call interference if the catcher touches the bat in his attempt to catch the ball. Conversely, it's interference when the batter puts himself in the catcher's way on a throw out to one of the bases. It's also interference when a runner hinders a defender's efforts to make a play, when a fair ball touches you, or when a spectator takes some action that impedes the progress of the game.

You're to call the ball dead when there is interference. At times the call will be made immediately; at other times it must be delayed until the play in which the interference occurred has been completed. One example can cover both cases.

Let's say that the batter interferes as the catcher is trying to throw out a runner who is stealing second. If there are two outs at the time, the call and the penalty come immediately; the batter is judged out. But if there are fewer than two outs, you must wait to see how the attempted steal ends. If it's successful, you should call the batter out and return the runner to first. If the steal fails, the interference is ignored.

The penalties for interference vary with the nature of the infraction. For instance, the batter is awarded first when the catcher interferes with him; if there is a runner on base at the time, and he fails to reach the next base on the play, he should be advanced to that base. When a runner interferes with a fielder, he's to be called out.

Obstruction is a specific type of interference. It occurs when a fielder who is not making a play comes in contact with a baserunner. The baserunner always holds the right of way unless the fielder is playing a batted ball. On noting obstruction, you should hold your call until the play is completed, because only then will you know the *degree* of the penalty to be assessed. Depending on how far you judge the runner would have advanced had he not been obstructed, you may want to award him one or two bases.

Regardless of where you're stationed in relation to a play, you should call interference whenever you see it. If you're at the plate and you see an interference that's missed by the field umpire, don't hesitate to speak up. Do the same if you're the field umpire. But since you're sure to be at a distance from the trouble spot, make certain of what you see before you act.

When working the plate, always be on the alert for the danger signs of interference. Watch out for the catcher who perennially crowds up to the plate. And watch for the batter who consistently reaches back with his bat; he may be trying to force an interference call by having the catcher touch the bat. And be ready for any batter dramatics on plays when the catcher must throw the ball out to a base; the batter is not allowed to move in any way that causes his bat or body to interfere with the throw. Likewise keep your eye on the batter when a runner is heading for the plate; the batter is entitled to remain in the box during the play, but he must not do anything to interfere with the catcher's attempt to put the runner out; above all, he can't leave the box in a way that will block the catcher.

Close Tags Tags that come as a runner is sliding into base can be especially difficult to judge. Your primary job is to position yourself so that you can see between the runner and the baseman. If you place yourself even slightly behind one or the other, the chances are that your view of the tag will be blocked.

You must also get on top of the play—that is, within a few feet of the bag so that you have a clear and closehand view of all the action. Often runners employ little body actions to avoid being trapped. Often the baseman bobbles the ball and has it out of his hands at the time the runner touches the base. You'll miss these crucial actions unless you're close to the bag.

Often the bag is touched and the tag made almost simultaneously; the actions come so close together that you really can't separate them. You'll help yourself greatly by watching to see which part of the runner's body is first touched by the ball. If the ball touches the leading part of the runner's body—a foot, leg, or hand that is in advance of the rest of the body—it's a clear out. But should the ball catch a trailing part—the trunk or an area high up the leg—then the odds are that the runner is safe.

As should be done at all times, keep your eye on the play until it's completely over. Then swiftly and decisively make the call. No early turning away, please. You'll likely miss some action that completely reverses your premature decision.

Rundowns You should never be left to work alone when, seeming to need two sets of eyes, you're trying to cover a runner who is trapped between bases. Your fellow official, once he's made his own call, should hustle over to lend a hand. He should then take one end of the rundown territory while you attend to the other.

The umpire at the end where the play concludes is the one who makes the final call. The man at the opposite end should say nothing unless his help is sought. The procedure saves the embarrassment of a shouted "out" from one end and an echoing "safe" from the other.

Advances Under certain circumstances, a runner may advance after a fly ball by a teammate has been caught. He's free to advance if he's touching the bag at the time of the catch. If he's taken a lead off the base, he may advance only if he retags the base after the catch. Again you seemingly need two sets of eyes to cover the action—one for the catch and one for the runner.

Your best bet here is to find a spot where both the runner and the defender making the catch are comfortably within your field of vision. The prime spot is one that's pretty well off the imaginary line running from the ball to the occupied base. Watch the catch. Then immediately switch to the runner's feet.

The chronological order of the play will be of help here. In turn, you should see the ball land in the defender's glove and then the movement of the runner. You can then be certain the runner is behaving properly. But if the order is reversed, the runner is advancing prematurely.

Umpire Signals

As a baseball umpire, you're fortunate as far as signals are concerned. In comparison to football officials, for instance, you're required to use just a handful. We've already talked about the ones used for strikes and balls, fair and foul hits, and safe and out calls. Shown in illustration 4 are those that remain for you to learn.

Three of the signals require a word of explanation:

• *Dead ball, immediately* (Figure 3): Used in situations such as a batter being hit by a pitched ball or a spectator touching a batted ball. Signifies that the ball is dead right now. As you extend both hands directly overhead, turn your palms so that they're facing forward. Be sure your fingers are fully extended.

4. Baseball Umpire's Signals

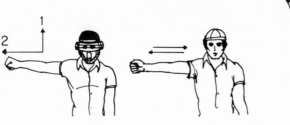

1. Strike

2. Player is out

3. Ball dead immediately as for batter being hit by pitch or batted ball touched by spectator

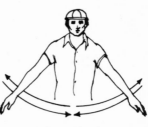

4. Delayed dead ball as for balk or catcher interference

5. Infield Fly

6. Runner is safe

7. Fair or foul ball

8. Foul Tip

9. Do not pitch and time-out

10. Play ball

From *Baseball Rulebook*, The National Federation of State High School Assn's

- *Dead ball, delayed* (Figure 4): Signifies an infraction for which you have the authority to ignore the penalty or award the bases after no further advances are possible. It's used for such infractions as a balk, an illegal pitch, interference, obstruction, or a fielder's use of illegal equipment in checking a ball. As shown, simply extend your left arm out to the side with clenched fist.
- *Infield fly* (Figure 5): Signifies that the infield fly rule is in effect. Clenched fist and arm straight overhead.

To repeat a point stressed in Chapter One, take great care to make your signals clearly and definitely. Time them properly, gesturing as soon as you're sure of your decision. Don't hesitate too long and give yourself a look of uncertainty. An extra burst of energy will serve you well on close calls; there's nothing like an impression of confidence and decisiveness to discourage an argument.

Umpire Equipment

The traditional outfit for the baseball umpire is a blue suit, black shoes, white shirt, dark tie, and blue cap. In recent years, following the lead of American League umpires, amateur officials have taken to wearing dark jackets and gray trousers. It's now also permissible to umpire in shirt-sleeves during particularly warm weather.

Depending on your league, you may or may not be required to wear a specific uniform. If not, you should still arrive in an outfit that looks as much like a uniform as possible. Also, you and your fellow umpire should agree to dress alike, wearing shirts of the same color and similarly colored slacks. If one wears a tie, the other should do the same. A like appearance will give you and your companion an official look and will make your job a degree easier. Above all, of course, your dress should be neat and clean. Women should always wear slacks rather than skirts for ease of movement and for an extra degree of leg protection.

When working the plate, you'll need several items of safety gear: A chest protector, a protective mask, and shin guards. Men are also advised to wear a protective cup. In addition, you'll need a ball sack, a ball-and-strike indicator, and a small whisk broom for clearing the plate of dirt.

You may use either an inside or outside chest protector at the plate. If you opt for the inside protector—which, as its name indicates, goes under your coat—always wear a T-shirt so that there is no direct contact with the skin. The inside protector is not worn with a dress shirt, and direct contact often causes rashes. Also, since you have no hiding places for your arms, you'll be wise to bring along a set of elbow and bicep guards. When dressing, be sure to adjust the chest protector to a snug fit that will keep it from slipping during the game. When the protector is correctly adjusted, it will shield your collarbones and will slightly overlap with the mask.

When wearing the outside protector, always take hold of its adjustment strap before each pitch. The strap is held in the left hand and lifts the protector up behind the mask and against the underside of your chin. Make sure that the protector directly faces the pitcher's mound. Properly lifted and faced, the protector will safeguard your torso and throat.

Both elbows should be tucked behind the outside protector, and your hands should not be visible beneath its bottom edge. With the inside protector, hold your hands with their backs facing away from you; if you are hit, the wrists will act as hinges and allow the hands to ride with the ball. No matter which protector you're using, never place your hands on your knees.

You'll undoubtedly have to buy your uniform, and depending on your league, you may be responsible for bringing along your own equipment. The equipment can be purchased through any sporting goods shop. You'll find that your original outlay will be on the heavy side—probably somewhere in the neighborhood of $200 at today's prices. But the investment will be a good one. With proper care, your gear should serve you well for years to come.

3. Football

DEPENDING ON THE LEVEL of play, two to seven officials may handle a football game. Two officials are commonly found in grade school competition. At the opposite end of the scale, seven work at the professional level, and six in college play. Some high school frosh and junior varsity games are assigned to a crew of three. Customarily, however, most games played by youngsters in their teens are supervised by four officials.

Because it's the one you'll most likely encounter, we'll concentrate on the four-man system in this chapter. It's a system that provides excellent coverage.

The Officials

The officials on the four-man crew are the *referee,* the *umpire,* the *head linesman* (often simply called the linesman), and the *field judge.*

One point must be made immediately about this foursome. In some sports the referee alone makes *all* calls while his fellow officials lend him a hand in a variety of ways. Not so in football. Here each official is in charge of a given area and holds certain responsibilities before and during the development of a play. Then as the play develops, responsibility for coverage and calls is shared. There must be this sharing, because no official coping with twenty-two players on the move can hope to see all that is happening.

The duties—individual and shared—of each man on the crew can best be seen when you try your hand at the mechanics of play coverage. Before going to the field, however, you need to know that whatever your officiating position, you'll hold some responsibilities in addition to those of coverage. Here they are now.

The Referee You're the senior official on the crew, the chief, and as such, you're responsible for the overall control of the game. Your fellow officials are able to make calls, but you're the one who signals all decisions to the sidelines and gives them their official stamp. You're also the man who settles all questions not specifically covered in the rules. Additionally, you hold a string of pre-game responsibilities that we'll be talking about later in the chapter.

The Umpire You're responsible for checking all player equipment prior to the game. Without exception, you're to disapprove all illegal equipment. Your association's rulebook contains a complete list of forbidden items and should be studied closely.

The Head Linesman The line-to-gain crew—the sideline unit that handles the chains and down marker—is in your charge throughout the game. It's your job to bring the chains in for measurements, to reposition the crew on first downs, and to supervise the shift of the chains to the opposite end of the field at the end of the first and third quarters.

The Field Judge Yours is the job of timing the game. If there is an electrical clock at the sidelines, you work with its operator to see that it's started and stopped at the correct times. If you're keeping the time yourself on the field, you routinely supply the operators of the scoreboard clock with information on the minutes remaining in a period. You also keep the referee informed of the time left in the second and fourth quarters.

5.

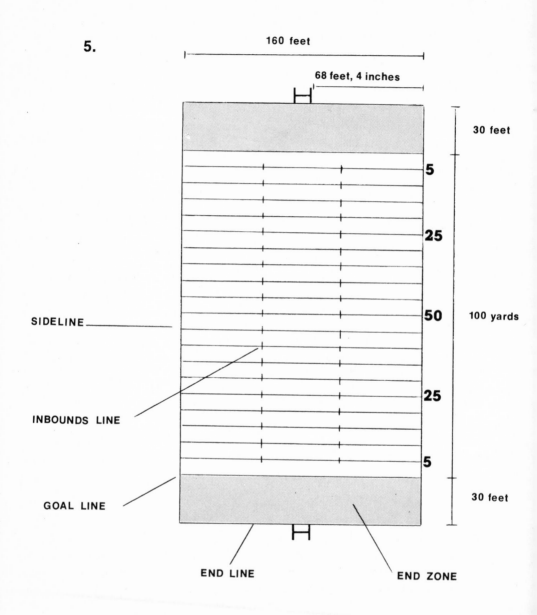

The Mechanics of Officiating

Now it's time to look at those procedures and techniques that enable you and your fellow officials to cover each play completely. Let's work first as the referee on plays that break from scrimmage.

The Referee: From Scrimmage As shown in illustration 6, your starting position is behind the deepest man in the offensive backfield. Set yourself off to his side so that you're at a good angle to view the coming play. If the ball is close to an inbound marker, your position should be to the wide side of the field. If the ball is out in the middle, pick the side that is away from the head linesman.

6.

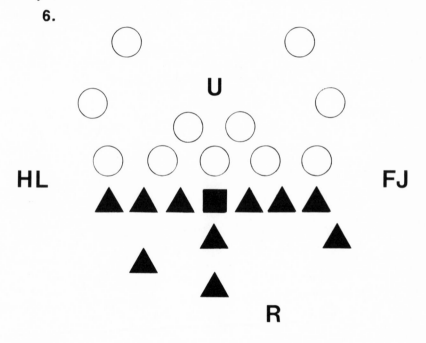

Make sure that you have a clear view of the ball. You should also be able to see as many of the backfield men as possible. Thus positioned, you're ready for your first job—to check that the play breaks cleanly without any illegal offensive backfield movement. You needn't worry about the men in the line. Nor about the offensive back in lateral motion. Linesmen and backs in lateral motion are the responsibilities of the umpire, the head linesman, and the field judge.

The Referee: Run Coverage When the play turns into a run, you trail the carrier, keeping the ball always in sight, and determine where forward progress stops.

As the play develops, don't be too quick in committing yourself to a movement towards the line or to one possible carrier. Remember that the initial moves of the offensive backs can fool you. Wait the instant necessary to see who's got the ball and where the play is going. A premature commitment can put you in the way of a reverse, a screen pass, or a fumble.

You must pursue the ball closely, but not too closcly; otherwise you may actually restrict your view as well as hinder the players should there be a backward pass or a reverse, or should the carrier cut back for running room. And don't pull in directly behind the carrier; his back can screen your view of some critical action on the ball. When the play ends, you should be behind and off to his side.

As soon as forward progress stops, whistle the play dead. Move to the ball immediately—if possible before or on the whistle—so that you can spot it (set it in place) for the next play. Your quickness here will help to cut down on any extra contact by the players. You'll also help matters if you promptly signal that you can see the ball and know the forward point of progress.

While you're following him, the carrier will sometimes outdistance you or will be screened from view by other players. This most often happens when he breaks into the defensive secondary. Another official should then take over for you, close in on the play, and whistle the action dead at the appropriate moment. Trail behind and check for illegal blocking away from the carrier.

The Referee: Pass Coverage Before any play breaks—and especially when a pass seems obvious—check the locations of the offensive backs, determining which are positioned as eligible receivers. Once the ball is snapped, stay with the passer and look for fouls against him. In your first days there will be a natural tendency to watch the ball sail away. Overcome it as quickly as you can. Keep your eyes on the passer until you see whether a charging defender makes an illegal contact. And don't turn away after a legal contact or when there promises to be no contact at all. You may miss some subsequent action of importance.

As the play develops, you must also check on the legality of the pass. If the passer breaks out of the pocket and runs forward, watch that the release comes while he's still behind the line of scrimmage. If there is a lateral or backward pass to a man who then throws the ball forward, make sure that the ball actually travels laterally or backwards.

If the pass drops incomplete, you or the umpire should move to the exact point where the ball was put into play. Mark it with your foot or beanbag marker and stand waiting while your fellow officials return the ball to you for spotting. The ball is customarily retrieved by the official closest to it. On long passes the officials should form a line for relaying the ball quickly back to the line of scrimmage.

If the pass is complete, the official nearest at hand will whistle the ball dead at the end of any postreception action. Hurry to the spot where the play ended. Check with your fellow officials for any infractions they may have seen and make any decision that may be necessary. Finally, spot the ball for the next play.

The Referee: Spotting the Ball As the chief official on the field, you're responsible for spotting the ball after every play. In actual practice, however, this usually becomes a shared duty with the umpire. The umpire customarily spots any ball that crosses the scrimmage line—either on a pass or run—while you take care of plays that end at or behind the line.

To insure an accurate placement, the man who spots the ball should first glance at the flanking official (the head linesman or the field judge) on the near sideline. It's the flanking official's job to track the play and then place one foot—well pointed—on the sideline stripe at a spot in line with the point of forward progress. He does the same thing on balls that go out of bounds. Any other official with a good view of the ended play should also assist in marking the point of forward progress with an extended foot.

Once that point is accurately determined, the ball is set in place with its forward tip against the farthest forward point of progress. If the ball is in the outer third of the field, it must be moved to the inbound line. A fellow official should assist by planting his foot and pointing it at the spot where the ball is to be placed.

No matter who spots the ball—you or the umpire—you take over once it's in place. You now (1) check the chains for the distance needed for a first down and, if necessary, ask the head linesman for the number of the next down; (2) announce the down and the yardage remaining to a first down; and (3) determine that the down marker is in place at the line of scrimmage and is showing the correct down number. Everything ends when you face the defenders' goal line and execute the *ready to play* signal; it's done with a short blast on the whistle and a simultaneous downward pump of your right hand. The offensive unit now has twenty-five seconds to launch the next play; the field judge counts off the time and you assess the required penalty if the play doesn't start on schedule.

Now for that next play, let's shift you to the umpire's spot.

The Umpire: From Scrimmage Your starting position on any play from scrimmage is in the defensive backfield, no closer than five yards behind the line, and no farther back than ten. Your primary job is to watch the interior linemen on both teams—and the defending linebackers—for blocking and use of the hands.

You'll find it impossible to watch every blocker and charger. And so on every play or at frequent intervals you should shift your position somewhat. Each shift will permit you to put the emphasis on a different group of players, keeping everyone honest in the course of the game. When moving to a new location, be sure not to pick a spot that interferes with any defensive back's view of the line or his movement on the play.

Before the play breaks, check the field judge's position. Ordinarily he stands at one end of the opposing lines, his job being to watch for such matters as encroachment, false starts, and illegal use of the hands. There will be times, however, when he senses that a pass—or knows that a punt—is in the works. He'll move off the line and take a position downfield for better coverage. You then must shift into his side of the field and, in addition to your own surveillance chores, take on his.

The Umpire: Run Coverage On runs, after checking the initial blocking in the line, follow the play. But do not concentrate on the carrier. Rather, watch the blocking going on around him and flag any fouls that you see. If the ball crosses the line of scrimmage, get ready to spot it.

The Umpire: Pass Coverage You share pass coverage responsibility with the head linesman and the field judge. In general, you cover passes down the middle while each flanking official takes care of balls coming into his side of the field. Naturally you're all free to help each other on the coverage.

Once you're checked the blocking as the play breaks, your primary responsibility shifts to watching for ineligible receivers and checking to see if the pass travels beyond the line of scrimmage. As soon as the play shows pass, move to the line of scrimmage, turn, and pick up the flight of the ball so that you can help rule on whether the ball is caught by a legal receiver. If the play is in your area, whistle the ball dead when the pass falls incomplete or when the postreception action ends. If you're screened from the play, let the official nearest at hand take care of the whistle.

It's time now to move to the head linesman's spot.

The Head Linesman: From Scrimmage Your starting position is at one end of the opposing lines. It should be about ten to fifteen yards from the lines themselves and outside the flanker back. Your line-to-gain crew is stretched along the sideline behind you. The field judge, unless he's off the line, stands directly opposite on the far side of the field.

You're to sight along the neutral zone—the area, that, defined by the tips of the football, stretches across the field between the opposing lines—before and at the break of each play. Your responsibilities are several. Before the play breaks, watch to see that there is no encroachment into the zone and no false start that pulls an opponent forward. At the same time keep an eye on a back in motion, alert to any premature break downfield. And don't forget to check the offensive backs to locate eligible receivers in case the play turns into a pass. Then as the play breaks, watch for illegal use of the hands on and by the receivers on your side of the field.

Your surveillance is shared with the field judge. You need only watch your side of the field, leaving him to his side. When the field judge moves off the line, extend your vision so that you can be of help to the umpire, who shifts his starting position and adds the neutral zone watch to his other duties.

The Head Linesman: Run Coverage When a running play goes up the middle, follow it along your side of the field and determine where forward progress stops. Stop in line with the end of the play, plant a foot firmly, and point your shoe tip at a spot directly in line with the forward tip of the ball. Hold your foot in place until the ball is spotted.

When a play comes to your side and gets beyond the inbound line, your view of the action is almost certain to be better than the referee's, and you should take over for him. Follow the carrier, whistle the play dead at the right moment, and then, as usual, mark the forward point of the ball with your foot. If the carrier travels out of bounds, mark the spot where he leaves the field and call for the clock to be stopped.

There are going to be times when the carrier comes right at you. Move clear of the action by stepping in a direction opposite his line of travel. While evading him, be sure not to take your eyes off the carrier. Keep him in sight at all times.

The Head Linesman: Pass Coverage As was said before, pass coverage is shared by the umpire and the flanking officials. You're responsible for covering the passes that come to your side of the field. Once a pass seems definite, move upfield with your receivers, tracking the ball so that you can settle on the intended receiver. If the ball goes to another area, don't drop out of the play. Stay with the action, pick up any infractions that the official responsible for the coverage might miss, and mark the spot where the play ends.

The umpire and field judge should lend you the same assistance on passes arriving in your area. Such cooperation guarantees that every pass play is well covered and controlled.

When the pass heads into your area, move to the point of reception as quickly as possible so that the play there will be clearly in your view. En route and on arrival be alert to all the problems that a reception can trigger. Is there illegal contact between the receiver and defensive back? Is there offensive or defensive interference? Has the ball been legally caught, or has it been trapped? If the catch is made at the sideline or deep in the end zone, is the receiver inbounds? Your answers will determine the results of the play.

The Head Linesman: Handling the Chains Regardless of your other duties on a play, you remain in charge of the line-to-gain crew. Whenever a measurement is needed, you're the man who must handle the chains and lead the crew onto the field. Here's the procedure you should follow.

On hearing the referee call for a measurement, have the chain tightened along its length from the rear stake. Next, grasp the link that is in the center of the yard line closest to the rear stake; this will allow the measurement to be made with the longest part of the chain, thus assuring maximum accuracy. You can hold the link between your fingers or attach a special marker clip to it. The clip is recommended—that way, if you drop the chain at some point during the measurement, the proper link won't vanish. (Some linesmen put the clip in place at the start of each series of downs to avoid a time loss.) As an extra precaution, set the down marker in the forward stake's spot at the sideline; there will then be no problem about returning the stake to its exact original location after the measurement.

With the chain in hand, run forward with your chainmen. Place the link in the center of the yard line when you're level with the ball. While you hold the link in place, the umpire takes the forward stake, stretches the chain taut, and places the stake alongside the ball. The referee supervises the final placement, checks it, and judges whether a first down has been made. The down is awarded if any part of the ball reaches the stake.

When the ball is short of a first down, the referee signals the distance remaining with his hands. Return the chain to your exact starting point. If the measurement on the failed down was made in the side zone or at the sideline stripe, the ball will have to be returned to the inbound line. The referee holds the chain at the forward tip of the ball and, assisted by you and the chainmen, trots it out to the line for placement.

In the event of a first down, you supervise the advance of the chains. See that the rear stake is placed in line with the forward tip of the ball. You must attend to the placement personally and not leave it to the chainman. Once the stake is in place, have the chain stretched taut. Finally, instruct the down marker assistant to set himself at the line of scrimmage with the correct down showing on the marker.

Now a final shift—this time, to the field judge's spot.

The Field Judge Your starting position is directly across the field from the head linesman's spot. Your surveillance duties before and at the break of the play are the same as his, as are your run and pass coverage duties.

As you know, you'll need to move off the line of scrimmage when a pass or a punt seems imminent. For punt coverage your best spot is about fifteen yards upfield. For pass plays, you may station yourself wherever you feel comfortable, with your positioning often being dictated by the pass patterns you've seen. There is little or no guesswork involved in recognizing a punt situation. But since an off-move reduces the amount of neutral zone coverage on your side of the field, you should not shift position for a pass unless you're pretty certain it's in the works.

The Field Judge: Timekeeping Duties You hold the prime responsibility for timing the game. No matter how heated the action, you must see that the game clock is started and stopped at the right moments. A close study of the rulebook is necessary to know those moments.

Though you're responsible for the clock, all your fellow officials should lend a hand here. For instance, the official who calls a foul should signal for the clock stopped as soon as the ball is dead; precious time will be lost if he has to seek you out to get the job done. The same goes for the official who is closest to an incomplete pass, a play that goes out of bounds, a made fair catch, or a score.

Special Plays

The work of all officials during the bulk of the game will be from scrimmage. There are moments, however, when special plays are put to use. They require a change in your starting positions. Let's look at them now.

Kickoffs Starting positions for the kickoff place the referee, the head linesman, and the umpire with the receiving team, and the field judge with the kicking unit. The referee and head linesman station themselves on opposite sides of the field in the vicinity of the deepest receivers. The station should be around the 10-yard line and about ten yards inbounds. From here both men can easily cover end zone and out-of-bounds kicks and any receptions that return the ball upfield.

7.

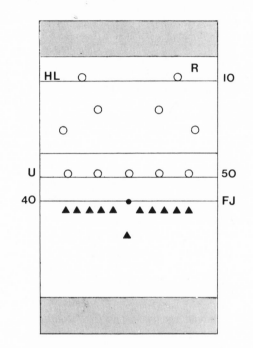

The umpire takes a position on the head linesman's side of the field. He stands just out of bounds somewhere between the receiving team's 45- and 50-yard line. He watches the five men in the forward wall. They must be within their 45 and 50 at the time the ball is kicked.

The field judge supervises the placement of the ball for the kick. He hands the ball to the kicker, instructs him to kick on the referee's signal, and remains with the kicker until the ball is on the tee. Then he moves to a position on the referee's side of the field, at the sideline at the kicking unit's 40-yard line. Once there, he checks that the unit is behind the 40. No player may advance beyond that line until the ball is kicked.

When both teams are set, each official raises an arm to signal that he's ready for the play. The referee starts the action by dropping his arm and sounding his whistle.

If the ball sails up the middle or shades itself to his side of the field, the referee takes over the primary coverage. He falls in behind the carrier and trails him upfield, just as he would on a running play from scrimmage. The head linesman moves up his own sideline and watches the action away from the carrier. These jobs, of course, are reversed on a kick that comes into the linesman's side of the field. And they're usually traded off when the carrier cuts from one side of the field to the other, outdistancing the covering official or causing him to become screened from the action.

Once the ball is airborne, the umpire and field judge track its flight upfield so that, should it sail out of bounds, they'll be able to help pinpoint where it left the field. They also study the blocking as the kicking unit moves upfield.

Now what if there's a breakaway run that brings the carrier beyond midfield? Depending on the side of the field involved, either the umpire or the field judge takes over primary coverage. The previously responsible official turns his attention to the action away from the carrier.

Depending again on the side of the field involved, the umpire or the field judge is also responsible for primary coverage on very short and onside kicks. Should there be a penalty that necessitates a rekick, the field judge supervises the reteeing of the ball at the new yard line.

Punts Let's continue with the kicking game, talking now about punts, or as they're often called, kicks from scrimmage. The starting positions for them are shown in the illustration below.

The head linesman takes his usual spot to the side of the opposing lines. The field judge stands downfield, ready to cover the deep receiver. The umpire shades himself to the field judge's side of the line. Before the snap, the duties of the umpire and the head linesman remain as they were for an ordinary play from scrimmage.

As for the referee, he stations himself slightly to the rear and side of the punter, staying at least five yards away from the man. As with pass coverage, he checks the onrushing defenders for illegal contact with the punter. Once that determination is made, he's to locate the flight of the ball. If the ball goes out of bounds while still airborne, he gets a bead on it, lends a hand in determining where it left the playing area, and handles the spot-

8.

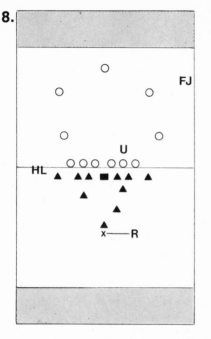

ting. Should the ball come down inbounds enabling a runback, he trails the kicking team upfield, watches the blocking, and prepares to pick up and cover the runner should the return be a long one. If the carrier doesn't manage a substantial runback, the referee hurries to the point where the play ends and takes over the spotting. The official closest to the action at the end of the play whistles the ball dead.

At the snap, the umpire moves to the neutral zone as he would on a pass play. If the punt is blocked, he and the referee cover the subsequent action and determine which team gains possession. Should the ball clear the line of scrimmage, the umpire turns and watches the action upfield, checking the blocking away from the receiver. He is particularly alert for—and in an excellent position to see—clips and blocks below the waist.

On the kick, once the ball clears the line of scrimmage, the head linesman hurries downfield to the point of reception. He takes over primary coverage if the ball is caught on his side of the field, trailing the runback until he whistles the ball dead, or on long returns, until he surrenders his coverage to another, better placed official. If the ball hits the ground inbounds and then bounces across the sideline, he marks the exact point of departure. When the kick sails out of bounds while in the air, he works with the referee in spotting the ball.

Stationed up with the deep receiver, the field judge takes on the same jobs as the head linesman on kicks that come into his area. Both officials are also responsible for enforcing the rules that surround a fair catch and a touchback; each man handles them on his side of the field; the field judge is responsible for them on kicks up the middle.

Goal Line Plays The starting positions on a goal-line play are much as they are for any play from scrimmage, and the presnap duties continue as usual. The field judge, however, will need to vary his position according to the number of yards remaining to the end zone. If the ball is between the 2- and 5-yard line, he should take his customary spot at the end of the opposing lines and then move to the goal line on the snap. But if the ball is less than two yards out, as pictured in the illustration, he should straddle the goal line right from the start; otherwise there likely won't be time for him to shift once the play breaks.

The field judge's presence on the goal line is vital, and the head linesman should join him there as soon as the ball is snapped. From their flanking positions, they're best situated to see whether a drive up the middle, a dash to the side, or a pass actually penetrates the end zone. Ob-

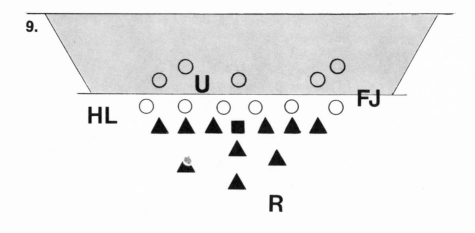

9.

viously, they're better placed than the referee who is watching a play that is moving across a line away from him, and whose vision is often screened by the plunging action that is the hallmark of goal line stands. As for the umpire, he's surrounded by blockers with the crucial action often taking place behind him.

All this is not to say that the referee and umpire will be chronically "blind" here. Any official is apt to be given a solid look at the play and, if certain of his decision, should blow his whistle and make the call. He should immediately signal the *touchdown* (both arms fully extended overhead) if the end zone is penetrated. No penetration requires the *dead ball* signal (one arm fully extended overhead).

Once the touchdown is signaled, the referee checks for penalty markers. If there has been no infraction to jeopardize the score, he makes everything official by resignaling the TD.

On plunges up the middle, there's sure to be a pileup of players. The flanking officials must watch the carrier closely. If he goes over the top, a determination must be made instantly as to whether he advanced the ball to a point above or beyond the goal line before his forward progress was stopped; if so, he's put six points on the board even if he is then thrown back. Should he dive low and disappear below a welter of heaving bodies, the referee must then close in on him and locate the ball. The key here is for the referee to move quickly and decisively, allowing little or no time for that extra squirming and battling that can alter the point where forward progress actually stopped.

The flanking officials need to be especially careful on plays that send passes or runs to the side. A special effort must be made to stay out of the way of the players. On passes, the official should move to the sideline if possible and step out of bounds while always keeping his eyes on the receiver. If the pass is right at the sideline or deep in the end zone, the receiver's (or the interceptor's) feet have to be watched; in high school and college, one foot must be inbounds at the time the ball is caught and brought under control. It's best not to be too close to a receiver or an interceptor who is operating near the sideline, the sideline-and-goal line, and the sideline-and-end line. The action of the feet is better seen from farther back.

Point-After-Touchdown and Field Goals The extra points after touchdowns can be scored in two ways—by a place kick for one point, or a run

10.

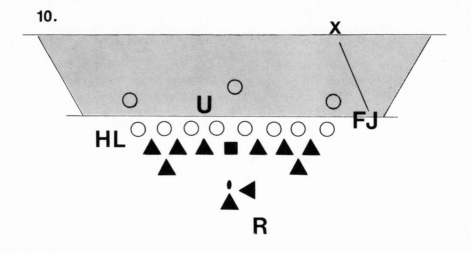

or pass for two points. When the PAT try is obviously to be a run or a pass, the starting positions are the same as for a goal line play. The positions for a PAT kick are shown in illustration 10.

The referee takes a position five yards or so to the rear and side of the kicker and holder. On the snap he moves directly behind the kicker so he can track the ball in flight and determine whether it passes between the uprights and above the crossbar. The field judge, who is stationed on the end line at a point several yards from the goal structure, lends a hand by watching the crossbar. If the ball clears the bar, he signals *thumbs up;* a ball below the bar earns a *no score* signal. The referee makes a successful attempt official with a TD signal. If the ball sails right or left of the uprights, he signals no score and indicates the side to which the ball sailed.

During the kick the head linesman watches the kicker and the holder, making the call if one or the other is roughed. The umpire is responsible for the action in the lines.

The starting positions remain the same for a field goal attempt, and the referee again moves behind the kicker at the snap. Up at the end line, the field judge watches the arriving ball in relation to the crossbar. The field judge's work on a point-after-touchdown is usually ceremonial because the referee is close enough to the goal to judge the kick without help. But not now. The field judge is almost directly beneath the passing ball while the referee, sometimes forty or fifty yards away, may not even be able to determine whether the ball reached the goal, much less passed above the crossbar. If the attempt is successful, the field judge signals touchdown. The referee verifies the signal by repeating it.

Handling Penalties

Fouls are bound to crop up in any sport. Because of its violent nature, football generates more than its fair share at times. All officials hold concurrent responsibility for sighting fouls and enforcing the appropriate penalties. Careful attention to the action and a swift response to fouls, especially those of a personal nature, can do much to keep the game moving smoothly and reduce the possibility of injury.

The usual penalties impose a loss of yardage (though flagrant acts of unsportsmanlike conduct can get a player disqualified or an offended team awarded a score), with the customary price tag in distance being five or fifteen yards. Five yards are marched off for minor technical infractions, among them encroachment and illegal shifts, while fifteen-yard assessments are reserved for fouls of a major nature. Most major fouls are personal in nature, and a few are technical. Representative of the major personals are clipping, illegal blocking, and unsportsmanlike conduct. Major technicals include an ineligible receiver downfield and a player's failure to wear the required equipment.

Though any official may call a foul, the job of officiating the penalty falls to the referee. Once a fellow official reports a foul to him, he takes over. For the beginning referee the handling of penalties always brings up three questions: (1) Where is the ball to be spotted before the penalty yardage is walked off? (2) When is the whistle to be sounded on penalties? (3) What's the exact procedure for officiating a penalty?

Putting you in the referee's shoes, let's answer each question in turn.

Spotting for Penalties Spotting is a headache because, depending on such factors as *when* and *where* the foul occurred, you can place the ball in any of four locations:

- At the spot where the ball was last snapped or free kicked. Technically, this is known as the *previous spot.*
- At the spot where the ball will next be put into play. Its technical name: the *succeeding spot.*
- At the spot where a run ended.
- At the spot where the foul occurred.

You can spot the ball without any problem on fouls that occur in the instant the play breaks. Always run the penalty off from the previous spot—the line of scrimmage for the play.

Nor do you have a problem on fouls committed between downs—in that stretch of time between the whistle that ends one play and the snap that triggers the next play. The ball goes to the succeeding spot, the line of scrimmage for the next play, and the penalty yardage is measured from there. Suppose a carrier is tackled on his 22-yard line, and a defender piles on after the whistle. Or suppose a defender encroaches before the ball is snapped at the 22. In either case the penalty is measured from the 22.

So far then, things are clear-cut. But the issue clouds when a foul occurs during a play. Before the ball can correctly be spotted, you'll need to know whether the foul came on a loose ball play or on a running play.

Passes, punts, and free kicks are designated as loose ball plays. All runs, of course, are running plays. But passes become running plays when legally caught by a receiver or an interceptor. Kicks turn into running plays when the receiving team collects the ball and begins a runback.

You're to penalize loose ball fouls from the previous spot. Let's say that the ball is on the offensive team's 40. When the quarterback drops back to pass, he's fouled in the instant after release, with the throw then falling incomplete. Spot the ball at the 40 for the run-off. It will also go to the 40 if the play is a punt and the kicker is fouled.

Fouls on running plays call for you to place the ball at the spot where the run ends. For example, a carrier advances to the opposition's 35 and is legally tackled. But five yards ahead—at the 30—either a defensive or offensive foul occurs. You're to measure the penalty *not* from the 30 but the 35. The measurement is also made from the 35 if there is a defensive foul somewhere behind the carrier, say at the 40. Were the penalty to be assessed from the 40, it would be effectively reduced by five yards and would be of advantage to the offending team.

There is one exception to this rule. Suppose that as the carrier is being tackled at the 35, an offensive foul occurs back at the 40. Now the ball is spotted at the 40—the point of the infraction—for the runoff. This time an unfair disadvantage to the offended team is sidestepped.

In addition to these general rules, here are some special points you'll need always to remember. Offensive pass interference brings the ball back to the previous spot. Defensive pass interference is assessed from the point of the infraction in college and from the line of scrimmage in high school.

Whistling the Foul The rule here is quite simple. The official who sights a foul should *never sound his whistle when the ball is live.* Once the ball is snapped, he's to leave the whistle alone and let the play continue. He's to flag the spot of the infraction with his penalty marker, note the number of the offending player (if possible), and carry on with his regular duties. When the play is over, he reports to you with news of the trouble.

The whistle, then, can be sounded immediately only during dead ball situations. For instance, if an official sees a clip after the play has been whistled dead, he can immediately sound off. The same goes if he sees encroachment before the snap.

Officiating a Penalty Whenever there is a foul, you and your fellow officials will need to follow a set routine in administering the penalty. It's a routine that has been developed over years of experience and should be followed religiously. It avoids confusion, handles the penalty efficiently, and restarts the game quickly.

As soon as the play ends, the official who sighted the foul signals time-out. Then he brings you, the referee, a full report on the situation: the type of foul, the time it occurred (during the play or after the ball was dead), where it occurred, the number of the offending player, and the team in possession at the time. If the foul took place on a pass or kick, he should tell you whether it occurred during loose ball play.

While the foul is being reported, you and your fellow officials have certain duties to perform. You immediately relay the reporting official's time-out signal to the field judge, who stops the clock. The umpire collects the ball. The head linesman warns his line-to-gain crew not to move the chains until instructed to do so.

Once you've got the report in hand, face the press box or the home team's sideline and give a preliminary signal for the foul. Next, move to the spot where the penalty is to be enforced, explain the foul to the captain of the offended team, and outline the options open to him—the down, the line of scrimmage, and the distance to a first down if he accepts or declines the penalty. Give him a brief moment to make his decision (long enough for him to think, but not long enough to delay the game or open the door to prolonged indecision); once he's given his answer, he can't change his mind.

When the captain's choice is obvious, be very brief with your explanation. If he doesn't answer, assume he agrees with you.

If the penalty is accepted, you need not step off the yardage unless the field is poorly marked. You'll move things along more quickly if you locate a point on the sideline at the correct distance from the enforcement spot and then stride to a point immediately in line with it. Tick off each yard line with an arm signal as you pass it.

On arrival, spot the ball and signal the penalty to the press box or the home team's sideline, pointing to the offending team. Watch as the head linesman brings his chain crew up to their new position. Check the down and the down marker. See that both captains are ready to play. Signal that the ball is ready and sound your whistle.

Should the penalty be declined, spot the ball at the new line of scrimmage. Again, signal the penalty to the press box or the home team's sideline, but wind things up with the *penalty declined* signal (a scissoring action of the arms).

There will be times when you're faced with multiple penalties by one team on a play. Handle them one at a time. Run off the distance for the first one, put the ball in place, and signal the infraction. Repeat the performance for each subsequent penalty.

And there will be times when each team fouls, and you end up with offsetting penalties. After spotting the ball, signal each penalty in turn, pointing to the team responsible. Then finish with the penalty declined signal.

Problem Calls

In a game involving hard body contact and twenty-two players any play can be a problem to call. But a number are exceptionally difficult because they produce more than the usual amount of scrambling action or because they demand an extra degree of officiating judgment. Here's a rundown of those that stand at the top of the list.

Fumbles Fumbles are a problem on two counts. First, they often occur near or right at the end of a play when the covering official is set to sound his whistle; the result can be an inadvertent whistle that kills the ball too soon and deprives the defenders of possession should they make the recovery. Second, with players scrambling after the loose ball, there's always the danger of confusion over the right to advance the recovered ball.

Only three simple and obvious suggestions can be made for the inadvertent-whistle problem. Always be on the alert for fumbles. Hold back on the whistle when you glimpse the ball leaving the carrier's hands before he's all the way down. Never go near the whistle if you're away from the play.

If you'll keep five simple rules in mind, you should have little trouble with the questions of possession and advancement, regardless of what confusing action may surround the play:

- When the fumbled ball is within the field of play, the team that has possession at the time of the whistle owns it.
- When a fumbled ball flies or bounces out-of-bounds between the goal lines while no player has possession, the fumbling unit retains possession, even if an opposing player is the last man to touch it inbounds; the same goes when opponents are in joint possession at the time it crosses the sideline. Should the ball go out of bounds behind the goal line, it belongs to the defenders.
- When the fumbled ball is recovered by the fumbling team, it may be advanced until whistled dead.
- When the fumbled ball is grabbed by the opposition before it hits the ground, it may be advanced.
- When the ball is taken by the opposition after it hits the ground, it may

not be advanced in college. It's dead at the spot of the recovery. It may, however, be advanced in high school.

Pass Interference This is the most difficult judgment call in the game because the technicalities and the action involved can bring on so many borderline situations. And since a tough call so often must be made on long passes when the action is in the open and in clear view from the stands, it can turn you immediately into the goat if your decision seems at all questionable.

A good call starts with the understanding that once a forward pass is in flight, all eligible receivers and all defenders have an equal right to go after it. Then while watching the ball come down, you have to keep two questions in mind: (1) is either player interfering with the other's opportunity to catch the ball, and (2) is either player "playing the man" and not the ball? If the answer is *yes* to one or the other, you've got pass interference on your hands.

Now some specifics must be added to modify your answer. Body contact is usually involved and can at first glance seem to be interference when it's actually not. Suppose that the receiver and defender crash into each other. Interference is not to be called if both men are in an equally advantageous position to take the ball and if each is playing the ball and not his man. The same goes if one man or the other is accidentally tripped while both are legitimately going after the ball.

On the other hand, interference is to be called if one man—either receiver or defender—tries to "run through" an opponent who has established an advantageous position to catch the approaching ball. Regardless of whether there is or is not contact, it's interference when one man stops or changes direction in an attempt to impede the progress of the other. The same applies if a player "blinds" his opponent by sticking a hand in front of the man's face.

Finally, it must be remembered that in one respect the rules governing pass interference differ for the offense and the defense. Pass interference comes into play for the defense only when the forward pass is airborne; this means that a defender may legally block a receiver before the pass is thrown (he may not, however, impede the receiver after the man makes his cut). Conversely, pass interference is in effect for the offense from the time the ball is snapped until its flight ends; at no time, then, may an offensive player upfield use his hands to push off an opponent.

You may not signal pass interference until the pass is thrown. Should you see interference prior to the pass, hold the penalty marker until the pass is in the air.

Late Hits Though not as difficult to determine as pass interference, late hits are judgment calls that can give you trouble. The keys to the call are the defending player's timing and apparent intent. If a player drives himself into or throws himself on top of an opponent after he's obviously heard the whistle or after the opponent has gone out of bounds, you should call the foul. But if he tries to avoid the opponent, tries to reduce the force of the impact, or otherwise attempts to protect the man, then there's no foul. Since football action is as fast and as hard as it is, these determinations can be tough to make at times.

Late hits rank high among the physical and emotional dangers in the game. They're among the chief causes of injury and are perhaps the leading reason for angry outbursts among opposing players. You can help to keep the game free of them by staying right on top of every play. Whistle the ball dead, not prematurely but quickly, in the instant that forward progress stops. And sound the whistle firmly and strongly. Then get to the ball fast so that your very presence warns off any hard-charging oncomers. You can also help matters by talking to the players, cautioning them that the ball is dead and that the carrier is down or out of bounds.

Late hit calls on out-of-bounds plays in front of the bench can be especially difficult. Your view is often screened by the welter of players and coaches there. And you need two sets of eyes—one for the contact and one for locating the out-of-bounds spot. All officials should quickly converge to lend you a hand. You should quickly mark the spot and then let everyone know you're there.

Clipping A clip is a deliberate or accidental contact with a player from the rear; the contact may be above or below the waist. Clips are most often seen on open field plays—kick runbacks, long runs, and pass receptions—when a blocking player throws himself against the back of a would-be tackler's legs.

Clips, however, are legal in certain instances. The carrier, for example, can be hit from behind. And any player may be clipped within what is called the "free blocking zone." This is the area stretching out four yards to either side of the ball and three yards fore and aft of the line of scrimmage.

The principal point you'll need to remember is that to be a clip, the contact must be *initially* from the rear. You'll run up against many instances in which the blocker throws himself against the front of an opponent, only to have the impact turn the man so that he goes down with his back to the blocker. If the action is caught during or after the turn, you can be fooled into thinking that you're seeing a clip. So your cardinal rule must be: Don't flag the action unless you see the contact right from the start.

In common with pass interference, clips produce more than their fair share of borderline cases, and your calls will have to be judgmental. Calls here should be made much on the basis of whether the blocked player could see and avoid the blocker.

While we're on the subject of clipping, please remember that crack back blocks have been outlawed in recent years. So have blocks below the waist on kicking plays. These blocks have been declared illegal because of their injury potential. Clipping is quite as dangerous, but there seems no way to get rid of it without outlawing blocking altogether. So keep your eyes open and consistently rule against it when you see it.

Roughing the Passer or Punter Once the ball is clearly airborne, a defender may not charge into the passer or the punter. But a number of mitigating factors have to be taken into consideration before you can make the call. For one, forget the flag if the oncoming defender tries to avoid the passer or the punter and then makes incidental contact. For another, forget it if his momentum carries him into the passer just after the release of the ball.

There's no foul if momentum carries the defender into the punter after blocking, or partially blocking, the kick. And don't call a foul for unavoidable contact when the kick is blocked, when the punter fumbles, or when he's running with the ball prior to the kick.

The flag, then, should be reserved for avoidable contact that is beyond the incidental. Because the kicker is especially vulnerable and because contact can be so easily avoided, any significant contact on a kick that goes unblocked should be called. But watch out for kicker dramatics. If at all talented, he can make a slight brush look as if he's just been hit by a train.

Throughout the Afternoon

Along with coverage responsibilities, each official must attend to several other jobs in the course of the afternoon. Some will have to be taken on as soon as you arrive at the field.

Pregame Duties If you're working as referee, six pregame duties will be waiting for you. They may be handled in any convenient order. You're to:

- Visit each head coach and provide him with a list of the officials' names.
- Tour the field with your officiating crew to see that it's properly laid out and marked. In particular, check for points that may later cause difficulty, chief among them faintly or irregularly chalked side-, goal-, and yard lines. Check, too, for hazards such as yard markers constructed of hard materials and placed too close to the sidelines. Correct all safety problems. If a nonhazardous problem (say, a poorly marked sideline) can be corrected quickly, order that it be fixed. Otherwise, decide how you and your fellow officials are going to officiate around it. So that there will be time for corrections, it's a good idea to inspect the field about a half hour before game time.
- Supervise a conference with your officials to review their duties—discussing officiating procedures and methods of cooperation—and check their equipment. The equipment includes whistles, watches, and record cards. If you and the officials are new to each other, the conference should really be your first order of business because it will give you your best chance for getting acquainted.
- If he has not already been named, designate the person who will operate the game clock; review his timing duties and the operation of the clock with him.
- Inspect the game balls and hand them over to the field judge.
- Introduce the team captains to each other and to your fellow officials

just before kickoff; supervise the coin toss and signal the captain's decision as to reception and choice of goal.

Now let's suppose you're the head linesman. Your pregame jobs are to:

- Collect the down marker and the chains. These items are usually supplied by the home team or the league. Their condition and the length of the chain should be checked.
- Meet with your line-to-gain crew. Usually the chainmen and the assistant who carries the down marker are supplied by the home team. Acquaint them with their duties and impress upon them the importance of never moving the chains (or the marker) without first receiving instructions from you; a mistaken or premature movement of the chains can cause much confusion when you're forced to locate the original spot to which they must be returned. You'll need to remind the youngsters of this point throughout the game; they can become quite forgetful in the excitement of the action.
- Assign the chainmen to their respective ends of the chain. Stress that they hold the chain fairly so that they do not, deliberately or unconsciously, give an advantage to their team.

If you're scheduled to work as field judge, your pregame jobs will be to:

- Check your watch and make sure it is working properly. If an off-field electric timer is being used, it, too, must be checked.
- Meet with the ballboy if more than one ball is to be used. Instruct him to work on your side of the field and always to keep his eyes on you so that there will be no delay in delivering the replacement ball to you when it's needed.

Should you be assigned to the umpire position, you'll need to visit both dressing rooms for a close check of player equipment, taping, and bandaging. All equipment must be in keeping with the rules. Nothing may be worn—from some personal item to the taping and bandages—that poses a danger to the player himself or to anyone on the field with him. If any item of equipment presents a problem, it's to be corrected immediately or the equipment is to be disapproved. You should complete your visits well before the warmup period so that there will be ample time for necessary adjustments. Once the adjustments have been made, check them.

Between Quarters The teams are given one minute at the end of the first and third quarters to change direction. Each official facilitates the change in the following manner:

The referee transfers the ball to the opposite end of the field, placing it at the appropriate yard line and at the proper distance inbounds; he then checks with the head linesman for down and distance. The umpire and the field judge move upfield with the teams to see that they comply with the rules in rearranging themselves; the umpire works with the defensive unit while the field judge handles the offensive squad.

The head linesman first checks the down and distance with the referee so that there will be no confusion in the placement of the ball and then leads his line-to-gain crew upfield. Before moving the crew, he marks the chain with his hand (or the clip) at the point where it crosses a yard-line stripe. He picks up the chain and, holding the appropriate link, orders the chainmen to reverse their stakes, then they proceed to the opposite end of the field. He places the marked link at the corresponding yard line and has the crew pull the chain taut. He then has them set their stakes, after which he places the man with the down marker and checks that the marker shows the proper down.

Halftime The intermission between halves usually runs for fifteen minutes. The field judge times the intermission and should start his watch as soon as the ball is dead after the expiration of playing time. When the time to resume play nears, he warns the officiating crew of the remaining minutes. The field judge is also responsible for holding the ball during the intermission.

As soon as the half ends, the head linesman moves his line-to-gain crew to their second half starting positions so they'll be ready when play resumes. At the end of the intermission, he reorganizes his crew and prepares them for the kickoff.

The officials should use the intermission for a conference to discuss any aspects of their work that will help improve the officiating in the second half. Problems that cropped up during the first half should be reviewed with an eye to avoiding or better handling them in the second half.

When play is ready to resume, the referee meets in the center of the field with the captains and obtains their second half options—choice of reception or kickoff and goal to be defended. The officials then take their starting positions for the kickoff.

11

FOOTBALL OFFICIALS' SIGNALS

Encroachment (Follows dead ball foul signal)	False Start. Illegal position or procedure Illegal forward handling	Illegal Shift. Illegal Motion.
Illegal Participation	Delay of game. Crawling.	Personal Foul.
Clipping.	Roughing the Kicker.	Unsportsmanlike conduct. Delay start of half.
Illegal use of hand or arm.	Failure to wear required equipment	Illegal forward pass.
Interference with fair catch or forward pass.	Ineligible receiver down field on pass.	Illegally kicking or batting a loose ball. Also for first touching of a kick.

From *Football Rulebook*, The National Federation of State High School Assn's

Incomplete forward pass-penalty declined- no play or no score.

Pushing, helping runner or inter-locked interference.

Touchback (Wave sidewise.)

Touchdown or field goal.

Safety.

Time out.

Official's time out— follows time out signal.

First down.

Dead Ball Foul. (Follow with foul signal.)

Ball ready for play.

Clock starts.

Loss of down.

Grasping opponent's face protector.

Illegal block below the waist.

Invalid Fair Catch Signal.

After the Game The referee's principal postgame job is to obtain the game balls and return them to the appropriate league or school official. The head linesman returns the chain and the down markers to the appropriate person or location. A few words of thanks are also in order—to the line-to-gain crew from the head linesman, and to the entire staff from the referee.

Signals

You'll need to learn a wide variety of hand signals. We've mentioned a number of them already. They and their companions can be seen in the accompanying illustration.

Whenever signaling, please remember the advice that was given at the start of the book. Execute the signals clearly and decisively, making sure that both benches and the spectators can see them. On fouls, be sure to signal twice—once prior to giving the options and then once again after the yardage has been run off or the penalty has been declined.

Uniform and Equipment

All members of the officiating crew wear the same style uniform. It consists of a black-and-white vertically striped shirt (the stripes are one inch wide), white tapered knickers and black belt, white socks over black stockings, and black shoes with black laces. The referee wears a white cap; his fellow officials wear black, baseball-type caps with white piping.

The shirts may be either long or short sleeved; whichever style is chosen, it should be worn by all members of the crew. In cold weather, jackets may be worn; they must be vertically striped in black and white.

So far as equipment is concerned, all officials should carry a whistle (you're advised to bring along an extra one in case of breakdown), a fifteen-by-fifteen-inch gold penalty marker; a plain-colored beanbag (white is preferred and sometimes required) for marking out-of-bounds spots and such; a game card and pencil; and two rubber bands. The rubber bands are connected and are used to keep track of the downs. One band goes around the wrist, with the second stretching from it and going around the appropriate number of fingers to indicate the current down.

In addition, the field judge will need to carry a watch for his timing duties.

4. Soccer

THOUGH IT HAS BEEN long known as *the* international game—and though it is said to be played and watched by more people than any other game in the world—soccer is something of a newcomer to the United States. It might well have gone without a chapter had this book been written twelve to fifteen years ago. But the times have changed. Largely because it welcomes players of all sizes and offers them a maximum of action with a minimum of dangerous body contact, amateur soccer is now played throughout the country and at all age levels from grade school through college.

When you become a soccer official, you'll work under one of two officiating systems. The choice of system will depend on your league or association. Each system has its own number of officials.

The Officials

If your league or association works under international rules, as set down by the Federation Internationale de Football Association (FIFA), three officials will be needed—a single *referee* and two *linesmen*.

12.

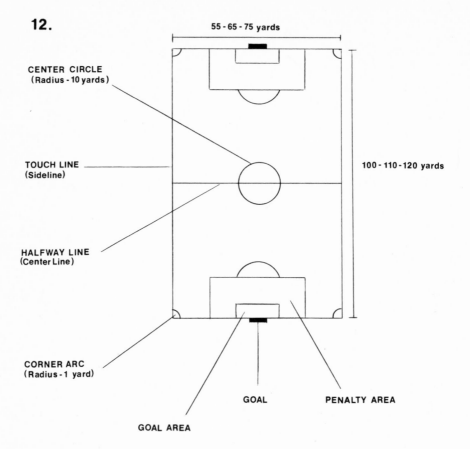

CENTER CIRCLE
(Radius - 10 yards)

TOUCH LINE
(Sideline)

HALFWAY LINE
(Center Line)

CORNER ARC
(Radius - 1 yard)

55 - 65 - 75 yards

100 - 110 - 120 yards

GOAL

PENALTY AREA

GOAL AREA

But, if your league is affiliated with such organizations as the National Collegiate Athletic Association (NCAA), a maximum of six officials may take to the field—two *referees,* two *linesmen,* and two *timekeepers.* Usually, one timekeeper comes from each school.

The single-referee system used by FIFA is to be found in most U.S. club, community, and youth soccer programs. The two-referee system is used in virtually all American collegiate games and is growing increasingly popular at the senior and junior high school levels.

We'll need to start with a comparison of the officiating duties under each system.

The Referee No matter whether you're working the one- or two-referee system, your duties and responsibilities as referee are the same. There is, however, a difference in their degree.

When working as the single referee, you're in complete charge of the game and make all calls. The linesmen assist you in several ways. Their basic task is to indicate when and where the ball goes out of bounds. They may also signal infractions to you. Their signals for infractions, however, are not official and are intended only as a help to your coverage of the game. It's up to you to acknowledge the calls and make them official. In the one-referee game, you also serve as timekeeper.

In the two-referee system, you and your fellow referee share the responsibility for supervising the game. Each of you holds equal authority. Each of you calls infractions and assesses penalties. Each of you indicates when and where the ball goes out of bounds. The linesmen do not even make out-of-bounds calls.

In fact, in the two-referee system, the linesmen are really nothing more than ballboys. Each carries an extra ball that can be put into play when the regular ball goes out of bounds. The action resumes immediately while the linesman retrieves the out-of-bounds ball.

Under both systems, your supervision of a game breaks down into a series of specific duties. You're to:

- Enforce all rules and make final decisions on all disputed points and on questions not covered in the rules.
- Start and stop play as the rules dictate. Play is stopped when the ball goes out of bounds, when a goal is scored, when there is an infraction, or when a seriously injured player must be treated.
- Determine—after conferring with the linesman if you're working the one-referee system—exactly where the ball went out of play and then supervise its return to action.
- Supervise all free kicks and dropped balls.
- Decide whether or not a goal has been scored.
- Control the entrance of players, trainers, and coaches to the field. No one—from substitute to coach—may come onto the field without first

securing your permission. You're also charged with preventing spectators from entering the playing area.

- Caution players for misconduct or unsportsmanlike behavior. In the language of international soccer unsportsmanlike conduct, which can range from objectionable language to fighting, is *ungentlemanly conduct.*
- Disqualify players for violent play or for persistent misconduct or unsportsmanlike behavior.
- Call an end to the game if the behavior of the teams or the spectators makes the continuance of orderly play impossible.
- Keep time if a timekeeper is not present.

In addition, you hold a number of pregame responsibilities. Tradition calls for you to arrive at the field at least thirty minutes before kickoff so that you'll have sufficient time for the work that needs to be done. On arrival, you should:

- Meet with your fellow officials to review officiating procedures, methods of play coverage, and any other matters that seem necessary for a well-called game. A few moments spent with the timekeepers to review their duties and check their equipment are also in order.
- Tour the field, checking playing conditions, all ground markings, and the goal and the net. The ball must also be checked to see that it meets rule specifications as to casing (leather or when the weather is wet, a plastic-coated leather), size (not more than twenty-eight inches and not less than twenty-seven inches in circumference), and weight (usually not more than sixteen ounces and not less than fourteen ounces at game time).
- Meet with the teams to clarify the rules if necessary and to answer any questions that the players may have.
- Meet with the team captains to give them their final instructions and to supervise the coin toss that decides kickoff and direction of play.

It's also your pregame job to check the players and make certain that their equipment—especially their footgear—meets rule specifications. At the same time be sure to check that no one is wearing anything that poses a danger to himself or his fellow players. All accessories that can scratch or gouge—wristwatches, heavy rings, earrings, and the like—must be removed immediately. So should necklaces; they have a bad habit of flying up into the face on sudden twists and turns.

The Linesmen As was said a few moments ago, you must be content with the job of ballboy if the game is being officiated by two referees. You and your fellow linesman station yourselves just outside the touchlines (side-lines) on either side of the field. You then simply trail the action so that you can place the extra ball at the spot where the regular ball goes out of bounds along your touchline.

For the one-referee game you also station yourself outside your touchline. But now, to repeat yet another point mentioned earlier, you stay abreast of the action so that you can signal when and where a ball in your area travels out of bounds. The signal is made by raising a flag directly overhead to full arm's length; you may use your hand or a handkerchief if a flag isn't available. You indicate the exact point of departure; the referee confirms your call and points to the spot you've indicated. Play resumes from there.

In addition to signaling the ball out-of-bounds, you must tell the referee which team is to restart the action. It's always the squad opposite the one that last touched the ball before it left the field.

You're responsible not only for balls out-of-bounds along your touchline, but also for those that get across the end lines on your side of the field. Balls that leave the field at the touchline are returned to play with a throw-in. For balls across the end line, play is resumed with a corner kick or a goal kick. More of the throw-in and these kicks later.

You may also, as was mentioned at the start of the chapter, assist the referee with signals for infractions. In particular, you should be ready to help him in sighting that always-difficult-to-judge infraction, offsides (it, too, will get further attention later in the chapter). In your early days as a linesman, however, the referee may want you to restrict yourself to out-of-bounds balls only. Later, on gaining officiating experience, you can begin signaling infractions.

The Timekeeper Your job, of course, is to track the game's playing time. Working with your companion timekeeper, you stop the clock on time-outs and then restart it at the appropriate moment. You may also be asked to keep score. Since soccer is a low-scoring game and since no other record of the action needs to be maintained, you shouldn't have any trouble handling the two jobs.

You'll work best with a stopwatch or with a timer that can be easily stopped. Whichever you choose, it should be large enough to be conveniently seen and should be placed so that both you and your companion can see it with equal ease. It's a good idea to have a backup watch or timer in case there's a breakdown.

In games without timekeepers, substitutes must report to the referee before joining the game. When you're on hand, they report to you instead. You then signal the referee of their wish to enter the field. The signal comes on the next time-out. Substitutes may not enter the game during time-in.

It's also your job to signal the end of the playing periods (there are two, each usually running forty-five minutes) and to time the intermission period between halves. The signal ending a playing period is given with a horn or a gun. Never bring along a whistle for this task. It can be too easily confused with the referee's whistle.

Now for some specific suggestions:

- Keep a constant eye on the referees so that you can stop the clock in the instant that a time-out is ordered. Time is called for a variety of reasons. It's always called when a goal is scored, when the ball goes out of bounds, when a penalty kick is awarded, and when an emergency occurs, such as the need to repair equipment or tend to a seriously injured player.
- When the play resumes, wait for the appropriate moment to restart the clock. The clock is not customarily restarted when the referee calls for time-in but when the ball is again in play. For instance, on a throw-in you're not to restart the clock while the thrower is holding the ball or sending it into the field. The restart comes when a player on the field first touches the ball. You'll need to study the rules closely for proper restarting times.
- In the excitement of the day, don't forget to time the intermission period, which usually runs for ten minutes. You're to notify the referees and the teams when there are two minutes left to the resumption of play. It's suggested that a separate clock be used for timing the intermission.

The Mechanics of Officiating

Your procedures for refereeing the action will depend on the system of officiating being used. Will you be working alone? Or will you be in the company of a fellow official? Let's look first at the one-referee system.

One-Referee System Here you use what is called the *diagonal* pattern of coverage. It calls for you to work along the diagonal line shown in illustration 13. At kickoff, you're stationed at the center circle. Then you track the flow of the action to points A or B, always remaining slightly behind the players.

Strong assistance must come from your linesmen if the pattern is to work. At kickoff each linesman positions himself at the edge of the center line on his side of the field. Each is them responsible for the touchline and the end line to his right as he looks into the field.

13.

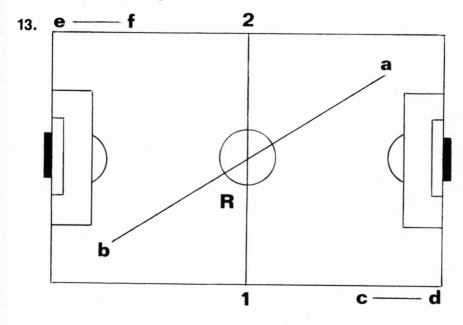

As play develops, a linesman joins you in tracking the ball when it is in his area. When you move to point A on your diagonal line, for instance, linesman 1 travels with you and at last arrives somewhere between points C–D. Back he comes to the center line when the players reverse themselves and head for and into the territory belonging to linesman 2. By the time you reach point B at the opposite end of the field, linesman 2 should be between points E–F.

The pattern requires the linesman to move slightly ahead of the action while you trail it. Thus the two of you always have the play surrounded. Traveling in the same direction, you've got it covered on both sides. And with one man consistently ahead of the other, it's covered fore-and-aft.

Only rarely will a linesman need to go into his companion's half of the field and then only for a few steps. At no time should linesman 2, for instance, travel to a spot opposite points C–D when you're at point A. His presence there is unnecessary because you've got the area under surveillance. He should be upfield at the center line, ready for the action when it flows back to him.

Two-Referee System Again a diagonal line is used, but this time it divides the field between you and your fellow referee. As is shown in illustration 14, one of you takes care of the field area, the touchline, and the end line in the unshaded zone while the other tends to them in the shaded zone.

Once the two of you begin to move with the action, you employ the *lead-trail* technique that's used in basketball. Here's how it works.

Let's say that you're referee 1 in the diagram. Remaining close to your touchline and moving slightly ahead of the action, you track the play as it travels through your area. Once the players near the goal, you cut left and head for the penalty area. The cut here keeps you on top of things in the event of a try for a point.

As for referee 2, he stays close to his own touchline, runs a course parallel to yours, and watches the action from his side of the field. At all times he remains to the rear of the play.

In this manner, with referee 2 trailing while you lead, the action is nicely surrounded—from either side and from fore-and-aft. Referee 2 is able to decide on plays that are screened from your view or too distant for

14.

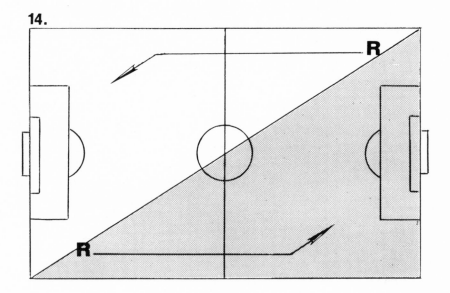

you to see clearly. He's also positioned so that he'll be in front of the action should the players reverse their flow.

If there is a reverse upfield, he takes over as lead official, tracking the action and then cutting towards his penalty area at the appropriate moment. You work the trail spot.

The lead-trail technique provides the action with excellent coverage. But it works well only if there is a great deal of cooperation between you and your colleague. The two of you should talk before gametime so that you each thoroughly understand your shared responsibilities and the manner in which certain anticipated situations are to be handled. For instance, you should both agree that, while the trail official is to be constantly on the lookout for fouls that are screened from the leading man, he should always defer to the lead man on actions that the two of you sight; this is because the lead official is usually better positioned to see an action. Finally, you both should agree to call as similar a game as possible so that the officiating does not change when the ball reverses direction.

Special Plays

Whether you're working a one- or two-referee game, the bulk of your time will be spent moving up and down the field within the two diagonal patterns just discussed. There are plays, however, for which you must take special positions.

The Kickoff The kickoff is used to start the game, to resume the action after a goal has been scored, and to open the second half of play. It is made from the center circle. The officiating positions for it are shown in illustration 15.

Figure A shows the positions in a one-referee match. The referee is stationed just outside the center circle while the linesmen are level with the opposing penalty areas and ready to accept the oncoming action.

In Figure B, the trail official stands inbounds near the center line, with the lead man positioned well downfield in the direction of the kick. The trail official supervises the kickoff, signals the timekeepers and the teams that play is about to commence, and then launches the kick by sounding his whistle. The two officials exchange duties when the kick is made in the opposite direction.

To ready the teams for the kickoff, place the ball at dead center in the center circle, take your starting position, and check to make sure that each team is in its half of the field. The kicking team may have players within the center circle, but all opposing players must be at least ten yards from the ball. The center circle has a radius of ten yards, so the opposing players have only to remain on or outside its boundaries to be safely positioned.

The kick comes on your signal. On being kicked, the ball must travel a distance equal to its circumference (twenty-seven to twenty-eight inches) before it is considered in play. The kicker may not play the ball a second time before another player has touched or been touched by it. Should he do so, an indirect free kick goes to the opposing team. We'll talk more of the indirect free kick and other penalty kicks later.

A goal cannot be scored directly from the kickoff. A goal here, incidentally, is pretty hard to achieve; the ball would have to travel fifty yards or so and then get past the goalkeeper. If there ever does happen to be a goal, reset the ball in the center circle and order the kick to be retaken.

15.

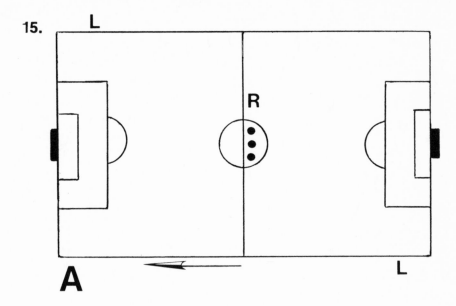

A

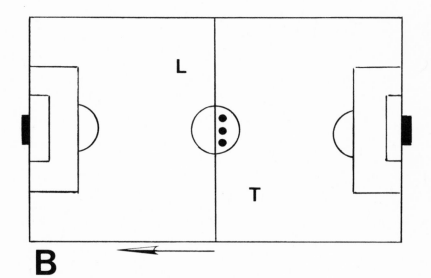

B

The Throw-In A throw-in restarts play after the ball has gone out of bounds across either touchline. It is made by a player on the team opposite the last one to touch the ball before it left the field. As you know, no player in soccer (with a scant few exceptions) can touch the ball with his hands. The throw-in is one of those exceptions.

In a single-referee match, the referee, of course, supervises the throw-in. The linesman on the opposite side of the field stations himself at a point on his touchline that will put him in front of the action should it flow in his direction. In a two-referee match, the throw-in is supervised by the official working the side of the field on which the out-of-bounds occurred; his fellow official picks a spot that will enable him quickly to take over either the lead or trail job once the ball is thrown.

When supervising the throw-in, keep close tabs on the man making the play. He must perform in a certain manner. He must hold the ball in both hands throughout, first carrying it back behind his head and then bringing it forward in an arcing movement to the point of release. His feet must be on or outside the touchline, and a part of each foot must remain on the ground until the ball is away. He should not attempt to score a goal directly from the throw-in. A violation of any of these rules sends the ball over to the opposition for a throw-in.

The ball is in play as soon as it's thrown, but the thrower may not handle it again until it touches or is touched by another player. When this rule is broken, you're to award an indirect free kick to the opposing team. It's to be taken at the spot where the infraction occurred.

The Corner Kick The corner kick and its cousin, the goal kick, come into play when the ball travels out of bounds across either end line outside the goal structure. The corner kick is taken by the attacking team when the defenders were the last to touch the ball while it was in play. Goal kicks belong to the defenders and are made when the attackers last touched the ball.

The illustration shows only the positions of the officials in a one-referee match, but they're identical to those taken when there are two referees. The referee stands close to point A of his diagonal line. He starts here at all times, regardless of the corner from which the kick is made. He then moves to the near side of the goal structure as he covers the action.

16.

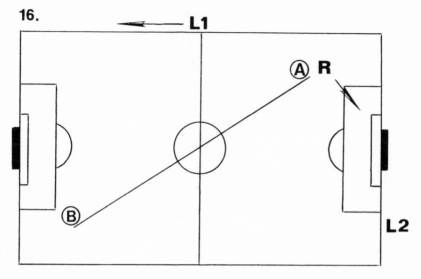

The linesman—in this instance, linesman 2—stations himself beyond the opposite end of the goal structure, often right at the edge of the penalty area. Positioned here, he's able to see any action that might be screened from the referee. Linesman 1 stands at the center line, ready to cover should the kick end with a surge upfield.

In the two-referee system the lead official takes the linesman's spot. The trail official starts at point A, then moves to the near side of the goal structure.

To supervise the kick, place the ball within the arc at the corner nearest the spot where the ball went out of bounds. Check the opposing players; as on the kickoff, they may not come within ten yards of the ball until it has traveled a distance equal to its own circumference. And watch the ball and the kicker; the ball must be stationary at the moment of the kick, and as usual, the kicker's not to play the ball again until it's touched by another player. The penalty for any violation here is an indirect free kick by the opposition from the point of infraction.

Incidentally, if there is a flagpost marking the corner, it may not be removed for the kick.

The corner kick is one of the most exciting plays in soccer because a goal may be scored directly from it. That often-confusing infraction, off-sides, is not in effect during a corner kick. As promised, more about off-sides soon.

The Goal Kick The positions for the goal kick are seen in illustration 17. In the one-referee system (Figure A), the referee stations himself at mid-field. Linesman 1 watches the kick from a point opposite the penalty area while linesman 2 stands up with the deep defenders so that he's in place should there be a hard attack by the kicking team.

In Figure B, the lead official works from a point about halfway between the penalty area and the center line, ready to move upfield on a hard attack. The trail man covers the kick from alongside the penalty area.

For the kick, the ball must be stationary on the ground within the goal area—at a point within the half of the area that is adjacent to the point where the out-of-bounds occurred. All opposing players must remain outside the penalty area and the kicker must send the ball out of the penalty area. If he is someone other than the goalkeeper, he may not send the ball to the goalie so that it can then be punted away unless it first clears the penalty area. Once the ball has cleared the penalty area, the kicker cannot play it again until it's touched by another man. A goal may not be scored directly from the kick.

What are your calls for infractions here? If anyone on either team—including the kicker—plays the ball before it leaves the penalty area, order the kick retaken. A rekick is also in order if the ball simply rolls to a stop before it clears the area. Should the kicker prematurely play the ball a second time, an indirect free kick goes to the opposing team at the spot of the infraction.

Handling Fouls and Penalties

When a player (or, in certain instances, a coach) commits a foul, you're to penalize him by turning the ball over to the opposition for a *free kick.* Any of three kinds of free kicks are awarded with the choice being dictated by the nature of the offense. The threesome are: the *indirect free kick* that's already been mentioned several times, the *direct free kick,* and the *penalty kick.*

17.

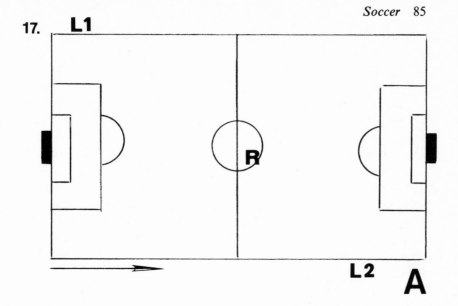

A

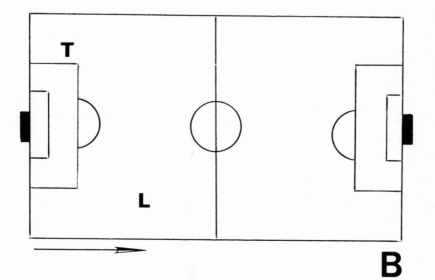

B

In general, the indirect free kick is awarded for technical infractions while the direct free kick is assessed for offenses of a personal nature. The penalty kick comes when a defending player commits one of the personal offenses while within his penalty area.

A goal may not be scored right from the indirect free kick, but the ball can be driven into the net for a point on both the direct and penalty kicks.

Indirect and Direct Free Kicks The rules that govern the kickoff, the corner kick, and the goal kick also apply to the indirect and direct free kicks. The ball is placed on the ground at the point of the infraction and must be stationary at the time it is booted. All players but the kicker must be standing at least ten yards distant; they're to be cautioned and moved back if they encroach on this distance. Nor may they move to the ball until it's traveled the distance of its own circumference. The kicker may not play the ball twice in succession.

There is one exception to the above rules. The opposing players may stand within the ten-yard limit if the kick is being taken nearer than ten yards from their end line. But they must stand on the end line itself between the goalposts.

Now let's look at the infractions that bring the kicks into play, starting with those for the indirect free kick. You're to award the kick when:

- A kicker illegally plays the ball a second time in the various instances that have been mentioned.
- A player is guilty of an obstruction other than holding (holding brings a direct kick). Obstruction shows itself in a number of ways. It's the call when a player in an effort to help a teammate reach the ball runs between an opponent and the ball. And the call when a player, who while not legally shielding the ball as he plays it, uses his body to form an obstacle for an opponent.
- A player is guilty of dangerous play. Dangerous play is any action that is apt to injure the player himself or those around him. High on the list of dangerous-play actions are: bringing a kicking foot above an opponent's shoulder, double kicking, and trying to head a ball that is below waist level.
- The goalkeeper carries the ball for too great a distance. Unlike the

other players, the goalie is allowed to take the ball in his hands. But he may not carry it more than four steps without bouncing it on the ground.

- A player charges another when the ball is not within playing distance. To be legal a charge must not only come when the ball is within playing distance, but must meet three other standards: (1) it must be a nudge or a shoulder contact when both the player and the opponent have at least one foot on the ground and the arms held to the body, (2) the charger must be in an erect position, and (3) both the charger and his opponent must be definitely attempting to play the ball.
- A player is guilty of misconduct or unsportsmanlike conduct. The offenses here can be quite varied. The player might try to distract an opponent by yelling at him. He might leave the field of play without your permission. He might constantly object to your calls. He might use abusive language with you or his fellow players. He might commit a serious foul.
- A player is offside.
- A player or coach is responsible for any of the following infractions: making substitutions or resubstitutions at the improper time or without your permission; entering the field without your permission; and persistently coaching from the sidelines after you've issued a warning.

Be sure to check your league rules concerning the sliding tackle, the action in which a player cuts in front of an opponent and takes possession of the ball by sliding into it. It's permitted in international play but has been outlawed here by the National Collegiate Athletic Association and calls for an indirect free kick.

Now for the direct free kick. It's the required penalty when:

- A player is guilty of intentional ballhandling—touching, striking, propelling, or carrying the ball with his hands or arms. Depending on your league rules, accidental ballhandling may be penalized or overlooked.
- A player trips an opponent. A trip need not be done only with the legs. It's a trip when a player throws an opponent by stooping or bending.
- A player kicks or knees an opponent or attempts to do so.
- A player charges an opponent in a dangerous or violent manner. Remember, for a charge to be legal it must be no more than a nudge or a

contact with the shoulder while both players have at least one foot on the ground and both arms against the body. Also, the charger must be erect at the time.

- A player charges an opponent from behind. There is one exception here: an opponent may be charged from the rear when he is deliberately obstructing. But that charge may be neither violently nor dangerously executed.
- A player jumps at an opponent. The word *at* is the key here. Jumping upward for the ball is legal even when body contact results. But no jumping towards a man to distract or startle him or otherwise interfere with his play. If sliding tackles are permitted in your league, no player may enter them with a jump.
- A player holds an opponent with his hand or any part of the arm. The player must also be penalized for holding if he waves in an opponent's face or extends an arm to interfere with the man's movement.
- A player pushes or attempts to push an opponent. No player may shove another away from the ball with hands or arms. Nor may he use the hands or arms to keep an opponent from the ball.
- A player strikes or attempts to strike an opponent.

The Penalty Kicks To refresh your memory, the penalty kick is awarded to the opposition when a defender is caught in one of the above personal fouls while within his own penalty area. It is actually nothing more than a variation of the direct free kick. But because of the location of the ball and the fact that a point can be tallied, it's easily the most exciting play in soccer.

Taken from within the penalty area, the kick requires careful positioning by the officials. The positions for one- and two-referee games are seen in the illustration.

In both cases the positionings are much the same. In each, one official (the referee or the trail man) watches to see that the kick is properly made and that no players encroach on the penalty area. His fellow official (the linesman or the lead man) checks for illegal movements by the goalkeeper and judges whether the kick ends in a goal.

With a goal at stake, you'll need to prepare carefully for the kick. First, no matter where the foul occurs in the penalty area, place the ball on the penalty kick mark. See that all players—except the kicker and the oppos-

18.

L1

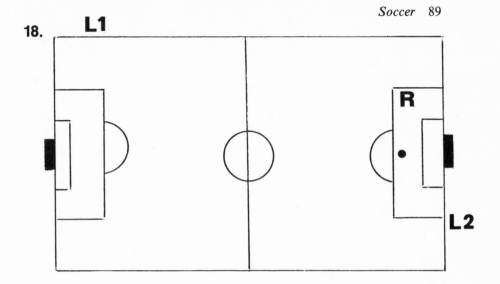

R

L2

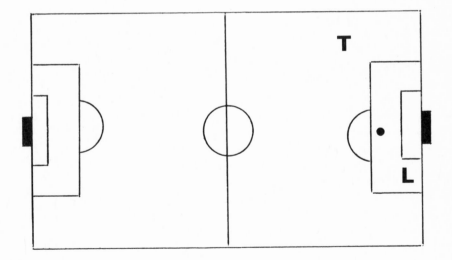

T

L

ing goalkeeper—are outside the area and at least ten yards distant from the ball. It's all right to let the players set themselves along the side boundaries of the area.

Check the goalkeeper. He must stand between the goal uprights with both feet on the end line. He may not shift his feet or move until the kick is made.

The kicker must send the ball forward in an attempt to get it past the goalkeeper and into the net. He may not drive it to the side so that a teammate can then rifle it into the net. Once the ball is in play (after it's traveled the distance of its circumference), the goalkeeper may move in any way to prevent it reaching the net.

The kicker, as usual, cannot touch the ball again before another player touches or plays it. But a special point must be remembered here. At times the ball will hit an upright or the crossbar and rebound to the kicker. He still may not play it.

You'll occasionally run into the situation in which the ball is kicked just as, or in the instant after, a playing period expires. If the ball goes into the net or touches the goalkeeper, the goal counts. If he deflects the ball and it is then driven into the net by another player, there is no score.

Problem Plays

Like all games, soccer has its share of difficult-to-judge plays. Here's a selection of those that rank high on the list of troublemakers.

Ball In or Out of Play The judging of whether a ball travels out of bounds is usually not a problem in a one-referee game because the linesmen are on hand and always alert to the call. But it can be a headache for two referees who must flow up and down the field and try to watch all facets of the action at once.

For the beginner the principal problem is the premature call, the mistaken whistle that comes because he *expects* the ball to go out of bounds. The only answer is to train yourself to withhold the call until you see that the ball has definitely left the field.

Always remember that for a ball to travel out of play, it must pass completely over a touchline or an end line (outside the goal structure), either rolling, bouncing, or flying across. If the ball hits the line itself and rico-chets back into the field, it's still alive and in play. By the same token, it's alive if it rebounds into the field after hitting a goal upright, the crossbar, or a corner flagpost. The ball is dead, however, when it flies out of bounds and then curves or is blown back into the playing area. So before making any judgment one way or another, always give yourself the extra moment to see how everything actually turns out.

Possibly your most difficult out-of-bounds calls will come when a player is right on the boundary line with the ball. Always base the call on the position of the ball and not of the player. Suppose that his feet are outside the touchline but his body is leaning inbounds for a header. The ball itself, then, is in fair territory and must be considered in play.

Under both international and NCAA rules, the ball is always in play until it goes out of bounds or until you whistle it dead for some reason. But there are differences between the two sets of rules that need to be re-membered. If you're working under international rules, the ball remains alive if it stays in the field after hitting either the referee or a linesman when he himself is inbounds. Under NCAA rules, it's dead whenever it strikes the referee; play is then resumed with a *dropped ball*. (Similar to the jump ball in basketball, in this play the referee restarts the action by dropping the ball between two opposing players. It's also used when the ball has become trapped or lodged between two players and cannot be kicked free.)

Handballing The problem here, really, is to remember your league's rule concerning the penalizing of accidental handballing. Players may touch the ball with any part of the body except the arms and hands—from the shoulders to the fingertips. Arm and hand touches are known as *handling the ball, ballhandling,* or just plain *handling.* All deliberate handling is to be penalized. Technically, accidental handling should also be penalized, but many soccer people feel that the penalties shouldn't be exercised be-cause they slow the game. Policy varies from league to league and some-times from age level to age level. Remembering the differences can be a headache for the official who works more than one league or age level.

You'll need to remember, too, the several exceptions to the handballing rule. A player, of course, must take the ball in hand for the throw-in. The goalkeeper may use his hands and arms to prevent a goal from being scored. And once the ball has entered the penalty area, the goalie's entitled to pick it up for the return to the field.

Further, a type of handballing is permitted in games for women and girls. They're allowed to protect themselves by crossing their arms in front of their breasts when chesting the ball. The touch is a legal one so long as the arms are tightly crossed and held right against the body with the hands fisted at the shoulders. The hands and arms must not be brought away from the body nor may they be used to deflect or aim the ball in any direction.

Goals For a point to be scored in soccer, the ball must enter the goal structure—that is, pass between the two uprights and beneath the crossbar.

Goal shots are pretty easy to judge when the goal structure is equipped with a backstop net. The fact is that the ball, if it's to land in the net, can't help but pass between the uprights and beneath the crossbar. But if your league can't afford a net, then there may be trouble. A ball can angle in so close to an upright or the crossbar that you'll be in for a difficult moment judging on which side it passed. The problem is worsened if you're minus the crossbar. Now you have to decide whether the ball was on a trajectory that would have carried it above or below the bar had the bar been in place.

Little advice can be given here other than the obvious: when you know a goal shot is coming, get into a position where you can see the goal clearly and then keep your eyes on the ball. Many referees feel that in the absence of the net or the crossbar, goals should never be awarded if there is the slightest uncertainty about them. Both teams will be treated with greater fairness if a policy of recognizing only undoubted goals is religiously followed.

In the event that the crossbar is missing, you're apt to run into the question of whether a rope should be substituted in its place. The recommended answer is no. The rope will likely cause more trouble than it's worth by sagging and reducing the size of the goal mouth. If the ball then skims over the top of the rope, it's sure to be argued that under ordinary circumstances it would have been within the goal mouth and so deserves to be counted as a score. There's a body of referee opinion that holds a game should be called off, at least in upper level competition, when the crossbar is missing.

Offside It would be pretty much of a cinch to score points in soccer if one or several attackers were allowed to come up to the defender's goal and cluster there awaiting the arrival of the ball. But this would be dullness personified for players and spectators alike, and the tactic would quickly turn an exciting game into no game at all. Hence, the difficult-to-judge offside rule.

At base, the rule states that no attacker may be ahead of the ball in the instant that it's kicked to him. Even one step ahead is enough to get him declared offside, the attack stopped immediately, and a free kick given to the opposition.

The rule itself is simple. What makes it difficult to officiate are its various technicalities. Most of them concern the times when offside is *not* to be called. They can cause endless trouble if you don't understand them thoroughly.

To begin, you must always remember that what counts is the position of the player at the time the ball is kicked, and not his position at the time he receives the ball. Once the ball is on its way, there's nothing to stop him from moving in front of it for the reception.

Next, in the interest of keeping the game going, you're not to penalize a player who is offside unless you think he is (1) interfering with the play of an opponent or is (2) seeking to gain some advantage by putting himself offside. It is this call in particular that makes an offside call so difficult. The call is a purely judgmental one and—especially when you're dealing with the possibility of player advantage—one that requires a sharp eye and a solid understanding of soccer tactics. It's sure to give you trouble in the beginning but should ease as you gain experience.

Finally, again in the interest of keeping the game moving, you're not to judge a player offside if any of the following five circumstances prevail: (1) the player is in his own half of the field, (2) two opponents are nearer to the goal than he, (3) the ball was last touched or played by an opponent, and (4) the player takes the ball on a drop or receives it direct from a throw-in, a corner kick, or a goal kick.

Fouls In a game as fast moving as soccer, you'll find it difficult to judge whether many actions are fouls or not. You can best help yourself here by asking: is the suspected player playing the ball or his opponent? If the answer is yes to the latter, you can safely call the action dead and award the appropriate penalty.

The rules of soccer are themselves much based on that question. From it come all the personal fouls that end in a direct free or penalty kick by the opposition. They're all acts in which the guilty player is obviously and intentionally attacking his opponent rather than the ball.

When the attacking team is closing in on the opposition's goal, a defender will sometimes intentionally foul his man in an attempt to take away the attackers' advantage. You must, of course, whistle the action dead for the penalty. But in your first days your problem will be not to whistle the ball dead too soon in your excitement. You must not stop the action if the halt will achieve what the defender set out to do—put the attackers at a disadvantage and perhaps deprive them of a score. Rather, make yourself wait until the play is over. In the meantime, signal that you've seen the foul by raising a fisted hand and calling "play on."

You must also keep a careful eye out for actions against the goalkeeper. He is especially vulnerable to charges by opponents and may be seriously injured if hit from the blind side. With only one exception— when he is obstructing—the goalkeeper may never be charged; nor may he be impeded or interfered with in any way when he has the ball. Charging him comes under the heading of dangerous play and calls for the immediate removal of the offending player. But you must watch to see that the charges are intentional and potentially dangerous. Accidental contacts of a minor nature are to be overlooked.

Finally, a warning system is used in soccer to keep flagrant misconduct at a minimum. You'll always carry two small cards—one yellow and one red—while on the field. The yellow card is flashed at an offending player to caution him against further improper play. A flash of the red card disqualifies him.

Soccer Signals

As a soccer official, you'll need to learn the arm-and-hand signals shown in illustration 19. You'll find that several (*offside, goal,* and *no-goal* among them) are identical to those seen in American football. All the signals, of course, should be learned thoroughly so that you can execute

19.

OFFICIAL SOCCER SIGNALS

1 GOAL	2 OFF SIDE	3 TRIPPING	4 STRIKING
5 JUMPING	6 HANDLING BALL	7 HOLDING	8 PUSHING
9 CHARGING VIOLENTLY. CHARGING — BEHIND.	10 GOALKEEPER CARRYING BALL	11 DANGEROUS PLAY	12 NO GOAL
13 BALL DEAD	14 TIME OUT	15 CORNER KICK Point to corner flag on side kick is to be taken	16 DIRECT KICK Forward under arm swing point direction of kick (1 arm)
17 INDIRECT KICK Forward underarm swing both arms point direction of kick	18 OBSTRUCTION Hit the chest with palms	19 PLAY ON	20 UNSPORTSMANLIKE CONDUCT

(By courtesy of the N.C.A.A.)

them without hesitation. They should be executed fully and deliberately so they can be clearly seen and understood by the players and the spectators.

Uniform and Equipment

In the United States the suggested uniform for officials consists of a white cap, a black-and-white vertically striped shirt, white knickers, black stockings, and dark boots. It's also possible to dress more in the style of the international referee, choosing a black shirt, black shorts, and black knee-length stockings; linesmen in international games usually wear dark shirts, dark shorts, and dark stockings. Depending on your league or the level of play, you may be able to substitute slacks for the knickers or shorts.

So that your footing is always secure, you'll need to wear studded shoes. Regulation soccer shoes are obviously your best choice here.

As referee, you should have two whistles, carrying one and keeping the other in reserve in case of a breakdown (be sure always to hand-carry your whistle and bring it to your mouth only when needed; you can be severely injured if hit with a ball while running with the whistle clenched between your teeth). If you're working without a timekeeper, you'll need two watches, again holding one in reserve. Bring along a notebook for recording fouls, scores, and the like. And don't forget a coin for the kick-off and choice-of-goal toss.

5. Basketball

MOST AMATEUR basketball games are officiated by a six-man crew. There is a growing tendency nowadays, however, to add a seventh man for an extra degree of coverage. In this chapter we'll concentrate mainly on the six-man operation, adding a brief section on the seventh man.

The Officials

The six-man crew is divided between floor and off-floor officials. The floor officials are the *referee* and *umpire;* in some leagues, they're both known as referees. Working at a table just off the court are two *scorekeepers* and two *timekeepers.* The rules permit the use of a single scorer and a single timer if they're experienced at their work and acceptable to the referee.

When a seventh man is added to the crew, he joins the floor officials as a second umpire.

The Referees and Umpire In actual play the referee and the umpire function as equals. Each covers the action, each calls fouls and violations,

97

each assesses penalties. Neither is authorized to over-rule the decisions of the other.

Should you be assigned to the referee's spot, however, you'll be considered the game's senior official. This is because you'll add a series of specific assignments to your general coverage responsibilities. The rules do not outline specific duties for the umpire. You'll be expected to:

- Rule on any matters of disagreement among the score and timekeepers.
- Make all decisions on points and questions not covered by the rules.
- Decide if a goal counts in instances of disagreement or question.
- Approve the score at the end of each half, signing the scorebook and making it official at game's end.
- Forfeit the game in accordance with the rules. Probably the greatest cause of forfeiture is a team's refusal to play when so instructed by a floor official. Flagrant misconduct by a coach can also result in a forfeit.

A number of your specific assignments must be attended to prior to gametime. You're to:

- Inspect the court and approve all markings and equipment there. Your check should include the backboard and the supports behind it, the basket itself, and the ball. At times you may find a floor that is somewhat oddly marked or that contains markings for other activities. If so, be sure to inform the visiting team of the unusual markings so that no one will be surprised and even momentarily put at a disadvantage by them.
- Check all player equipment. Have the players remove any item of personal or game gear that is dangerous to themselves or the other competitors. Jewelry of any type is not to be worn. Likewise, casts, braces, and guards of any sort may not be worn at high school level if made of a hard material. Nor may a player wear any equipment that is unnatural and designed to give him an unfair playing advantage by increasing his height or reach.
- Designate which of the four off-court personnel are to function as the official scorekeeper and official timekeeper (the remaining two will serve as their assistants). Their signaling devices should be checked to make sure they're in good working order and not confusingly similar in sound. It's a good idea to review your floor signals with the keepers and

to remind the scorekeeper never to place an entry in the scorebook when he's in doubt about it but to get in touch with you and let you settle the matter. You'll also need to designate the official scorebook and timepiece.

- Meet with the coaches and team captains to confer on any playing and officiating points in need of explanation or clarification.
- Inform both teams when the clock comes to within three minutes of game time. At the intermission you must also alert them when there are three minutes left to the resumption of play.

Though it's not required by the rules, a conference with your fellow official should be the first order of business on arrival at the arena. Discuss the manner in which the two of you hope to officiate the game. Settle all questions that come up on the specifics of handling given situations. You may find that you each have slightly different ways of doing and seeing things; if so, talk about them and settle on whatever compromises are necessary to insure that you work smoothly together.

Both you and your fellow official should time your arrival so that you can be free to take the floor at least fifteen minutes before game time (some associations want you out there twenty minutes ahead of time). You're officially in charge of the game from the time of your arrival on the floor until the moment when you approve the final score at game's end.

Though all the pregame duties belong exclusively to the referee, the umpire should lend him a hand in every way. Right from the start, long before the opening toss at center, the two of you should be functioning as a team.

The Scorekeepers Each school provides a scorekeeper. Unless the referee designates otherwise, the man from the home team serves as the official scorer, with the representative from the visiting squad acting as his assistant. They work together not only to keep track of the score but also to maintain a running record of the game. That record must include:

- Successful field goals.
- Points scored by each team.
- Successful and unsuccessful free throws.
- Personal and technical violations.

20.

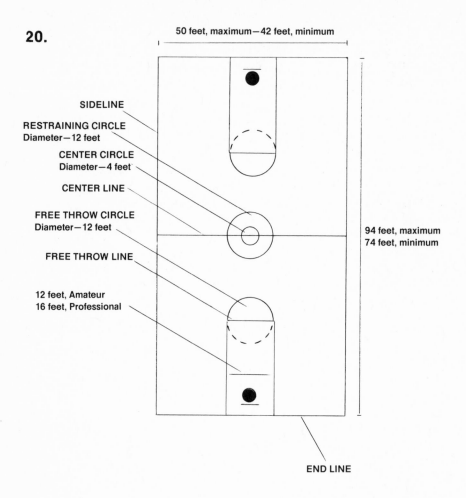

50 feet, maximum—42 feet, minimum

SIDELINE

RESTRAINING CIRCLE
Diameter—12 feet

CENTER CIRCLE
Diameter—4 feet

CENTER LINE

FREE THROW CIRCLE
Diameter—12 feet

FREE THROW LINE

12 feet, Amateur
16 feet, Professional

94 feet, maximum
74 feet, minimum

END LINE

• The number of time-outs. Additionally the scorekeepers must notify the nearest official at hand when the limit of time-outs permitted a team has been reached. Teams are usually allowed five time-outs in a regulation game, plus one in each extra period of play.

Each scorekeeper is given a scorebook or appropriate paper forms for his entries. The scorebook held by the official scorekeeper is the game's official book and comes from the home team. Whenever an entry is made in it, the assistant scorer watches and double checks to see that all is correct. Should the scorers disagree on any point—say, the number of a player responsible for a foul—or discover some discrepancy in the game record, they must notify the referee and then follow his lead in righting the matter. Likewise, when they fail to see a foul signal clearly, they must immediately contact the referee for a clarification.

When at all in doubt, the scorekeepers should never make any sort of entry on the basis of their own judgment. Their record of the game is the official one. It must be accurate to the nth degree. Especially important is the record of the team points scored. Should there be a discrepancy that cannot be resolved by the referee, the record in the official scorebook must be accepted as final, no matter how strongly some may suspect that it's incorrect.

Scorers use a horn, a klaxon, or a gong to attract the floor officials' attention. One point must be kept uppermost in mind here: when calling an official, never interrupt the action, but always wait until the ball is dead. The scorekeeper's audio signal should differ from that of the timekeeper and should in no way resemble the floor official's whistle. Otherwise, it can easily cause confusion.

The Timekeepers Again, each school provides a timekeeper. And again, unless otherwise designated by the referee, the official timer comes from the home team, with the visiting team representative assisting him. The timekeeping duties in basketball are the same as those in virtually all sports. You (1) stop and start the game clock, (2) time the duration of time-out periods, and (3) time the intermission between periods.

Many games today are timed with an electric timer. If the arena isn't blessed with this efficient piece of equipment, both timekeepers should have stopwatches. To avoid an argument if the watches don't show precisely the same time in close or tied games, the one carried by the official timekeeper is understood to be the official watch and is designated as such by the referee prior to game time. It's always good practice to bring along a spare watch or clock in case there's a breakdown along the way.

As a timekeeper, you'll need to keep two points in mind. First, the mechanics of officiating call for a floor official to sound his whistle *and* raise his arm when he wants the clock stopped. The clock must be stopped immediately. But don't depend solely—or even mainly—on the whistle as your signal to act. Too often the arena noise will drown it out. So never let your attention wander from the officials. The one signal that's always sure to come through is the upraised arm.

Second, from time to time you'll be asked to help determine whether a try for a point or a field goal was in flight before time expired at the end of a period. If the period ended while the ball was in flight, then the goal counts. So keep your eyes open.

Certain rules govern the restarting of a stopped clock. As a timekeeper, you must have them down so pat that they're second nature to you. Fortunately they're few in number: (1) on jump balls restart the clock when the ball is legally touched by one of the jumpers; (2) on throw-ins start when the ball touches or is touched by a player inbounds; and (3) ditto for missed free throws.

You must be equipped with a device for signaling time to the floor and the crowd. The usual device is a buzzer. It cuts very efficiently through the crowd noise. If you can't be given a buzzer, then insist on a device that differs from the scorer's horn and the floor official's whistle. Again the idea is to avoid confusion.

Court Mechanics

In basketball the mechanics of officiating are known as court mechanics. They involve a wide variety of procedures and techniques for play coverage but are basically built around the lead-trail system. The system calls for one official—the lead man—to stay in front of the action as it flows along the court while his partner—the trail man—brings up the rear. When the players change direction, the officials trade off the lead and trail spots.

21.

22.

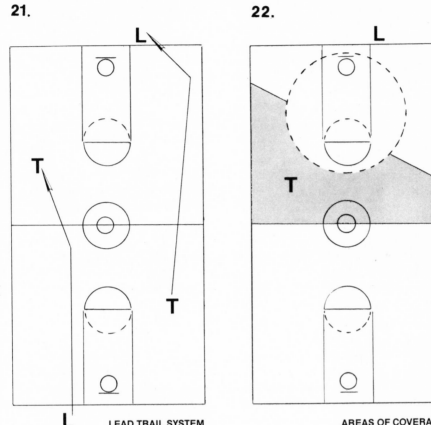

LEAD TRAIL SYSTEM

AREAS OF COVERAGE

As shown in the illustration, the officials keep the action surrounded by moving along opposite sidelines. On parallel courses they've got the play covered from the sides. Leading and trailing, they have it in sight fore and aft.

When you're the lead man, you should move to a position just out of bounds at the end line whenever the ball comes under the basket. Your spot should be near the basket and on your side of the court. The trail man should stop near his sideline at some point between the center circle and the free throw circle. The exact point chosen will depend on the play; he'll want the spot that gives him the best view of the action.

Once you're in position, each of you holds primary responsibility for a given piece of territory. As pictured, your areas are divided by an imaginary line that runs diagonally across the court. As the lead man, you're responsible for the unshaded area. You cover the action under the basket, along the sideline to your left, and in most of the forecourt.

As for the trail official, he's responsible for the shaded area. He must also watch the flight of the ball to the basket and signal if the shot is successful.

There is, however, an area of shared responsibility (it's shown within the broken circle). You're both to watch the always-critical action around the free throw line, in the free throw lane, and at the top of the key so that it is constantly given double coverage. Additionally, the two of you should assist each other in any way possible and should call any violation or foul that you see, regardless of whether it occurs inside or outside your areas of primary responsibility.

When the ball changes possession and the players sweep upcourt, you and your fellow official instantly trade jobs. He leads and finally takes a position at the opposite end line. You trail to a spot that gives you the best view of the action under the basket.

After every foul, the officials change sides, and each man crosses to the opposite side of the court. There are two reasons for the shift. First, it varies the game for the officials and thus contributes to their alertness; without it each man would be forced to operate under the same basket at all times. Second, it saves one man from continuously working near the sideline adjacent to the team benches. As any official will admit, it's the thankless side of the court.

The lead-trail system is simple to describe. In practice it demands unending cooperation between the officials and constant physical and mental adjustments on the part of each man, and so it's anything but easy to master. Study, long experience, and a willingness to learn from your mistakes are vital to mastery. The following suggestions will be of help in starting you along the road to a skilled performance:

• Whether leading or trailing, always stay on your side of the court. Neither wander nor unthinkingly follow the action over to your companion's side. Should you do so, the play will no longer be surrounded. You'll always be where you belong if you remember that when leading, the near sideline should be at your right; when trailing, it should be at your left. A simple formula should be kept in mind at all times: *lead right and trail left.*

- Be constantly on the move, always looking for the best spot from which to view the action. It's fatal to stand still for any length of time. The players are sure to screen your view of the action.
- Your best viewing spot is the one that enables you to see the ball itself and the players adjacent to it. Thus positioned, you're able, as officials say, to "look through the action."
- When you're the lead man on a fast break, you may need to run at full speed to stay ahead of the action. Resist any temptation to take your eyes off the action and look to your point of destination. Stay with the action; it's far more important to see what's going on than to arrive up-court ahead of the players. On slower breaks you should be able to back-pedal much of the distance.
- To stress again a point made earlier, be ready to assist your fellow official at all times. In particular, remember to call any foul or violation that you see, no matter where it occurs. Of course, be certain of what you see before you take action. No guesses, please.

Special Plays

While the bulk of your time will be spent working within the lead-trail system, there are three plays that call for you and your fellow official to take special positions. The plays are (1) the jump ball, (2) the throw-in, and (3) the free throw.

The Jump Ball The jump ball is used to start the game, to open a new period, and to retrigger the action after certain infractions and after the ball, as it's apt to do from time to time, has lodged itself in a basket support or an overhead fixture. Standing midway between two players and slightly to their sides, the official tosses the ball straight up. The jumpers go after it with each man trying to tap it to a teammate.

If you're working as a referee, you'll administer the play at the start of the game or a new period. The jump here is made within the center circle.

23.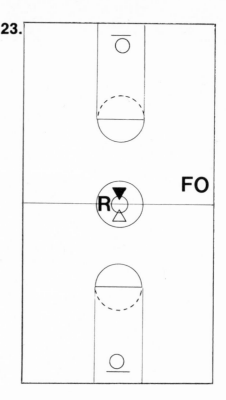

Start by positioning yourself in the circle with the two players so that you're facing the scorer's table. The umpire—the "free official"—stations himself opposite you and about six to eight feet inbounds from the scorer's table. Leaving the jumpers to you, he watches the remaining eight players.

You now have two jobs—to toss the ball correctly and to see that the jumpers go after it in accordance with the rules. To be tossed correctly, the ball must be sent straight up so that both men have an equal opportunity to reach it. And, regardless of the players' jumping ability or their height, it should always be tossed level with or above the basket rim.

The rules prohibit the jumpers from touching the ball until it attains its full height. You must always avoid a low toss. A low-tossed ball sometimes drops so quickly that the players have no chance to tap it. Just as often, it forces them to move so quickly that they foul by striking the ball while it's still rising.

You can best send the ball straight up by splitting your stance comfortably, planting your front foot firmly, and launching the toss from somewhere between chest and eye level. Most officials recommend the eye-level toss. When the toss begins at or below the chest, there's the danger of an arm swing that will send the ball away from one or both of the players.

If the toss proves to be inaccurate, either you or the free official may order it to be retaken with the call coming from the first man to sight the problem. Should you be the one to see the ball heading off course, immediately sound your whistle. Often, standing to the side as he is, the free official is better positioned to see the toss go awry.

A caution: When making the toss, be sure not to hold your whistle in your mouth. You're especially vulnerable to a hit or a brush by an arm as the jumpers go up. There can be severe damage if you're struck in the mouth while gripping the whistle between your teeth.

And a second caution: There will be a natural tendency to back away as the jumpers rise. Stay right in place until the ball is tapped away. If you back off too soon, you can be easily hit from the rear and injured by a charging player.

In seeing that the jumpers play in compliance with the rules, you must keep your eyes open for four possible infractions. Watch that (1) each man keeps at least one foot within his half of the circle and that neither player (2) hits the ball before it peaks, (3) catches the ball before another player touches it, or (4) leaves the circle before the ball is legally touched.

For his part the umpire watches for four infractions among the players outside the circle. He's on the alert to see that no nonjumper (1) enters the circle before the ball is tossed, (2) changes his position before the toss, (3) breaks the plane of the circle with his foot before the tap, or (4) positions himself between two opponents unless they occupy adjacent positions when the teams line up for the jump.

Once the ball is tapped, the umpire almost invariably becomes the lead official. He's automatically in position to lead when the ball travels to his right; he immediately moves upcourt and finally takes a position at the end line. On balls to his left (they would automatically put the referee in the lead spot), he leads until the referee can get into position at the end line. At that time he drops back into the trail spot.

Though the referee supervises the jump at the start of the game or a period, he is not necessarily the man in charge on other occasions. The jump is then handled by the official who calls for it. The official must then always stand facing the scorer's table so that his signals can be clearly seen there. The jump is to be taken from whichever of the three court circles is closest to the point where play stopped.

When the play is made in one of the free throw circles, it is supervised in the same way as the center jump, with the free official customarily taking the lead on the tap. There is one exception here, however. If the tosser is in the circle with the end line immediately to his right, he becomes the lead man on balls tapped to the right. This is because he has just a few steps to travel to the line.

The Throw-In Made by a player who tosses the ball inbounds from a boundary line, the throw-in is used to restart the action after play is stopped for a violation call. Violations, which are distinct from fouls, are infractions involving illegal movement, illegal ballhandling, and the failure to observe certain basket, court, and time restrictions; high on this list is causing the ball to go out of bounds. The throw-in is also used to retrigger things after time-outs, certain fouls, successful field goals, and free throws.

In general, the throw-in is made from the boundary line where the ball went out of bounds or from the spot closest to the point of an infraction. On an out-of-bounds call, it's handled by the team opposite the last one to touch the ball while it was still alive. (If there were simultaneous touches by opposing players, the action is to be restarted with a jump ball.) Following other infractions, it goes to the offended team. After successful field goals, it's made from the end line by the team that has been scored upon. It may be from the end line or the division line in the wake of free throws. (Check your rulebook for details.)

The responsibility for supervising throw-ins is pretty equally divided between the two floor officials. In those moments when you're working the lead spot, you administer all end-line throw-ins in the front court, plus all those along the front court sideline to your right as you face the basket. On switching to the trail position, you handle the ones in the back court and along the front court sideline to your left as you face the basket.

To insure the widest court coverage possible, the officials should station themselves to either side of the player making the throw-in. Thus stationed, the two of you will be able to keep an eye on the end line, both sidelines, and the division line. The technique is known as *boxing in* the thrower. The illustration shows how it works.

Figure A illustrates a throw-in from the front court end line. The lead official stands to the left of the thrower while the trail man is stationed upcourt—and several feet inbounds—to the thrower's right. On handing the ball to the thrower, the lead official backs off several feet along the end line for a wider look at the action to come.

Examples of throw-ins from the right and left sidelines of the front court are shown in Figures B and C. Again the administering official is to one side of the thrower and the free official to the other.

It was said earlier that you should always work on your side of the court and not intrude on your fellow official's side. The throw-in pass poses an exception to this rule. There will be times when the two of you will need to cross over to reach your new positions quickly. The maneuver is used only when the throw-in is made from the right side of the front court in relation to the team's line of travel. It's seen at work in the two instances shown in illustration 25.

The cross over enables you to move quickly to your new positions while maintaining a wide view of the action. But care must be taken to time the move so that both sidelines remain always covered. There is one spot that is usually not recommended for the cross over—the right sideline between the front court end line and an imaginary line that extends to the sideline from the free throw line. The crossover here can be awkward because of the limited amount of space available. In your pregame meeting, you and your fellow official should decide whether or not you wish to risk the maneuver in this area.

Throw-ins must be administered carefully. Start by whistling the clock dead and raising one arm overhead for time-out. Signal the violation or foul to the scorer's table; no signal to the scorer's table, however, is necessary for balls out of bounds. Clearly name the team that is to take the throw (this is done by calling the color of the team jersey) and indicate the team's direction of travel by extending your arm with your hand open. Finally, designate the exact spot where the throw-in is to be made.

24.

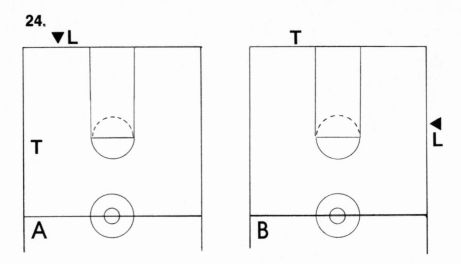

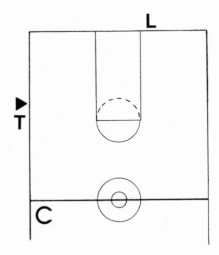

25.

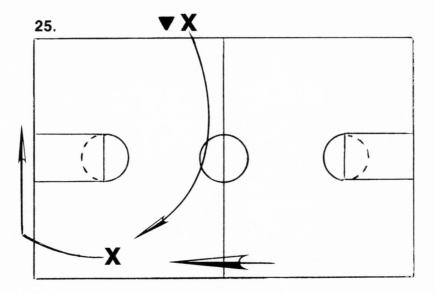

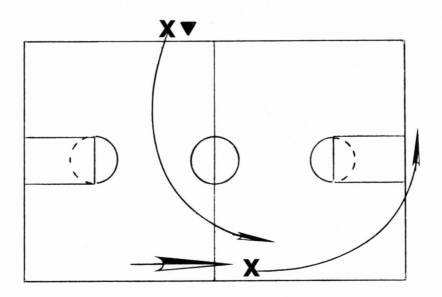

Following certain infractions, you must designate a player to make the throw-in. It's customary to select the man that the team wants for the job. But designate him only if he's close at hand. Otherwise, to avoid a delay, name someone else. In those instances when you need not designate a thrower, the ball may be assigned to any player on the inbounding team.

Once the signals are out of the way, hold the ball in readiness. But do not hand it to the thrower as soon as he takes his position. First check to see that your fellow official is ready for the coming action. Check also for any substitutes who may be waiting to enter the game. Wave them in.

Hand—do not toss—the ball to the thrower. He now has five seconds to put it into play. Start a silent but visible count of those seconds by making a chopping action with your right hand at waist level. One chop per second. Hold your position until the ball is inbounded or until the five-second period is up. As soon as the ball is inbounded and touches a player, signal the clock to start.

As the administering official, you're primarily responsible for covering the thrower and the players nearby while your fellow official handles the players outside the immediate vicinity. As you watch your man, be alert to see that he does not (1) leave his designated spot when attempting the throw, (2) break the plane of the boundary line with any part of his body, (3) bounce the ball on or outside the boundary line, or (4) touch the ball before another player does so after the inbound.

Two final points: First, the throw-in that follows all successful goals and most free throws (we'll talk about the exceptions in a little while) is not administered by an official. The team that has been scored upon, without waiting for you, takes the throw from the end line. The player making the throw-in is permitted to roam all along the line as he looks for a spot to inbound the ball. He may also pass the ball along to a teammate who then inbounds it.

Second, the lead-trail system, as you know, calls for the officials to exchange jobs after every foul. This procedure has an effect on the administering of postfoul throw-ins. The official who sees the foul calls time-out and sends the appropriate signal to the scorer's table. Then he switches positions with his fellow official. The fellow official supervises the throw-in.

The Free Throw The free throw is the penalty assessed for a variety of fouls; fouls are personal and technical infractions that, ranging from ille-

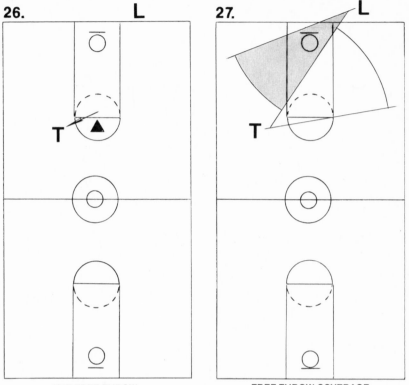

26.　　　**L**

27.　　　**L**

THE FREE THROW　　　　FREE THROW COVERAGE

gal body contacts to unsportsmanlike conduct, are considered to be of a more serious nature than violations. The ball goes to a member of the offended squad. Standing at the free throw line, he is permitted to try for a point by throwing the ball to the basket without being contested by the opposition.

Depending on the foul and the circumstances, the offended team is awarded one or two free throws. The team gets one free throw for a technical foul that's nonflagrant and two if it's judged to be flagrant. The same goes for personal fouls. However, should there be a nonflagrant personal foul on a man in the act of shooting a goal, he's given only one throw if the shot is successful. If he misses the shot, he's got two frees coming.

Several precise steps are involved in administering a free throw. First, on sighting the foul, whistle the ball dead, call for time-out with an upraised arm, and point your free arm, palm down, at the offending player's hip. Naming him by number and team, step to the player so that you can inform him of the nature of the infraction and, if the trouble has been caused by too much emotion, bring him under control. Then move towards the scorer's table. As you do, signal the foul, call the team's color, and hold up the number of fingers that will indicate the offender's number.

This procedure should be followed not only on fouls that result in free throws. It's also to be used on fouls that bring a throw-in.

At the time the whistle first sounds, your fellow official should come to a dead stop and watch the surrounding players. Once you've reported the foul, you take his position while he retrieves the ball. This constitutes the exchange of positions that comes after every foul in the lead-trail system.

Ordinarily, you administer the free throw when you find yourself in the trail spot. Move to the free throw circle and take a position between the free throw line and the basket; the lead man carries the retrieved ball to the end line and holds it there for the moment. Look to the scorer's table to double check that there is no confusion over the call. If there are substitutes waiting, call them in. Check to see that the players are distributed correctly along the lane spaces to either side of the free throw lane. The players from opposing teams should occupy alternate spaces. If the throw follows a personal foul, the spaces facing each other at the end line must be occupied by the offended team's opponents.

When all is in readiness, gesture for the ball, hand it to the shooter, and move off to his left, stepping slightly to his rear. While keeping your eyes on him, begin the silent but visible count of the ten seconds that he now has to make the shot. Count off each second by extending your arm with the palm of your hand down. Also, while backing off, signal the number of free throws to be taken.

The illustration shows how you and the lead official divide your areas of responsibility during the free throw. From his position beneath the basket, the lead man watches for player violations along the lane to the shooter's left. You watch for violations along the lane to the shooter's right. In addition, you must watch the shooter himself to see that he doesn't step over the free throw line or out of the free throw semicircle during his attempt. Finally, you need to follow the flight of the ball to see if the attempt is successful.

When watching the players along the lane, you and your companion must make sure that, prior to the throw, no offensive or defensive man (1) leaves his lane space, (2) touches the marks dividing the spaces, (3) violates another player's space, or (4) steps across the plane of the lane line. Additionally, check that no defender tries to distract the shooter by shouting or waving his arms.

If you sight an offensive infraction at any time after handing the ball to the thrower, sound your whistle and stop the play. Unless the team has another free throw coming, the opposing squad gets the ball out of bounds for a throw-in. No point is scored on the free throw.

Should you sight a defensive infraction, however, leave the whistle alone. If the free throw is not successful, call the infraction and award a substitute free throw as a penalty. If the throw is successful, forget the infraction and let the game proceed.

What happens if both teams commit an infraction in the same instant? Whistle the ball dead immediately. If the throw is successful, no point is awarded. Unless another try is upcoming, restart the action with a jump ball in the free throw circle.

Though they may seem to do so in the first days of your officiating, fouls only rarely occur in exactly the same instant. When they come in blinding succession, try to separate them in your mind and determine which one came first. It's the one that takes precedence. Experience will help you learn to place "simultaneous" fouls in their actual order.

When a false double foul occurs (a personal foul by a member of one team follows a personal foul by a member of the opposition before the clock is restarted), the mechanics for handling things must be altered. One official administers the free throw for the first infraction while his fellow official, accompanied by the player offended on the second foul, moves upcourt to the opposite free throw circle. Once the first free throw is made, the ball goes to the second player. If the second man makes a basket, a throw-in follows by the opposition from the end line. When the shot is missed, the ball is in play under the basket.

The mechanics must also be altered after a technical foul. The official who makes the call administers the free throw on his own. The second official stands at the intersection of the division line and either sideline. Following the free throw, the ball goes to him. He supervises the throw-in the offended team uses to restart the action.

Signals

As a basketball official, you'll need to use more than twenty hand signals. Some are to be flashed individually. Some must be flashed in combination.

As stressed elsewhere in this book, take great care to master the signals thoroughly, practicing them until they can be flashed automatically. On the court always signal clearly and decisively. On close calls give the signal an extra bit of energy so that you communicate the impression of being absolutely certain of your decision; the additional effort here will do much to avoid arguments.

Four Problem Calls

In common with all games, basketball has its fair share of problem calls. They all involve body contacts. They're problems because in the midst of heated and fast action it can be difficult at times to judge whether the contacts add up to fouls. And if the contacts are illegal, it can be just as difficult to judge, again because of the swift-flowing action, which players should be charged with the foul.

Let's look now at four situations that top the list of problems and consider how they should be handled. On the court you'll need always to keep two basic points in mind. First, for a contact to be illegal, it must be of sufficient severity to endanger the offended player or put his team at a disadvantage; in the interest of keeping the game going, incidental contact should be ignored. Second, if momentarily bewildered over who is guilty in an illegal contact, ask yourself one question: Who bears the greater responsibility for the contact?

Rebounding With a scoring opportunity hanging in the balance, the game is sure to be especially hot under the boards. You can count on much body contact as the players go for the ball as it rebounds off the backboard. Your swift and firm reaction to unnecessarily hard contacts can do much to lessen the risk of serious player injury that's always present here.

Both you and your fellow official are reponsible for calling rebounding infractions. When working the trail spot, you're also responsible for following the flight of the ball and judging basket interference. The lead man should concentrate solely on the rebounding action and ignore the flight of the ball.

Incidental contact is common during rebounding action. It should be ignored. Remember, call only contact that affects the game by endangering an opponent or putting his team at a disadvantage—but call it quickly.

The following examples should give you a good beginning idea of the kinds of calls you'll be making.

A player takes a legal position for a rebound (both feet on the floor, set for the play, and not illegally impeding an opponent). An opponent interferes with him by pushing from the side, charging from behind, or looming to his front with an unnaturally extended body position. A foul must be called on the opponent.

A shooter jumps high as he sends the ball to the basket. On dropping to the floor, his forward momentum carries him into the back of a defender who has taken a legal position for the rebound. The defender, perhaps stumbling forward, is hindered in making his play. Though the contact is accidental, the shooter is to be charged with a foul. If his shot was successful, the goal counts because the contact occurred after the ball was airborne and had no bearing on where the ball went. Had the contact occurred prior to release, the goal would be discounted.

A player goes into the air and taps the rebounding ball. Before the tapper leaves the floor, a defender takes a legal position to handle the next rebound. The tapper comes down, makes contact, and pushes him away. Again, the contact is unintentional but must be regarded as a foul. Again, the tally counts if the tap was successful.

You'll help your "rebounding cause" greatly if you always stick to three basic policies:

- Call rebounding fouls from the start of the game. Don't be lenient in the opening moments. Leniency is almost sure to convince certain players that they can get away with some pretty rough play.
- If you glimpse any unnatural movements or unusual body positions

28

BASKETBALL SIGNALS

1 — Start clock

2 — Stop clock or do not start clock

3 — Stop clock for jump ball

4 — Beckon substitute when ball is dead and clock stopped

5 — Stop clock for foul

6 — Point(s) scored (1 or 2)

7 — Bonus situation (for second throw drop one arm)

5 — Stop clock for foul
8 — Pushing or charging — follows Signal 5

5 — Stop clock for foul
9 — Illegal use of hand — follows Signal 5

5 — Stop clock for foul
10 — Technical foul

5 — Stop clock for foul
11 — Blocking — follows Signal 5

5 — Stop clock for foul
12 — Give 8 or 9 Then Give — Player Contol Foul

5 — Stop clock for foul
13 — Holding — follows Signal 5

For free throw violation: Use Signals 2 and 18

For basket interference: Use Signals 16 or 14 and 6

From *Basketball Rulebook*, The National Federation of State High School Assn's

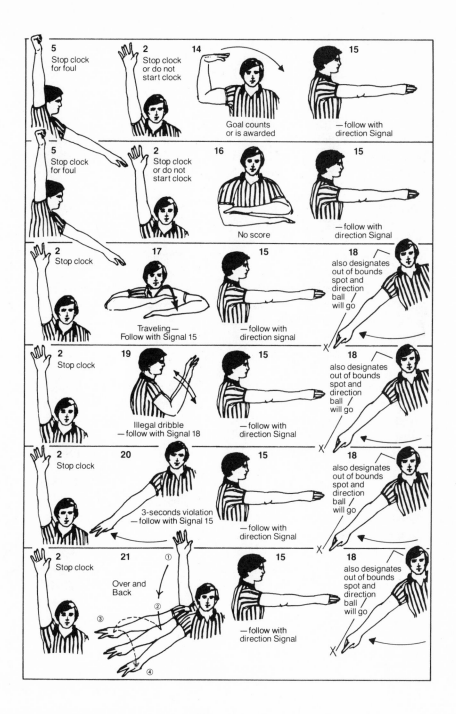

5 Stop clock for foul

2 Stop clock or do not start clock

14 Goal counts or is awarded

15 — follow with direction Signal

5 Stop clock for foul

2 Stop clock or do not start clock

16 No score

15 — follow with direction Signal

2 Stop clock

17 Traveling— Follow with Signal 15

15 — follow with direction signal

18 also designates out of bounds spot and direction ball will go

2 Stop clock

19 Illegal dribble — follow with Signal 18

15 — follow with direction Signal

18 also designates out of bounds spot and direction ball will go

2 Stop clock

20 3-seconds violation — follow with Signal 15

15 — follow with direction Signal

18 also designates out of bounds spot and direction ball will go

2 Stop clock

21 Over and Back ① ② ③ ④

15 — follow with direction Signal

18 also designates out of bounds spot and direction ball will go while the players are in the air, you can be fairly sure there has been holding, charging, or pushing somewhere in the action. But don't call the foul on suspicion alone. Rather, look more closely at the action. Then go to the whistle as soon as you actually see the next illegal contact.

• If you're the lead official, don't allow yourself to be drawn in too close to the rebounding action. Your view of the action will be better if you back off slightly, especially on shots from the outside. But remember, *back off*. Don't turn even slightly away from the action.

Blocking and Charging *Blocking* is defined as illegal contact by a defender against an opponent; the opponent may or may not have the ball at the time. *Charging* is illegal contact by a player "in control"—that is, the dribbler himself or any man on the offensive unit.

The definitions are simple enough. But when two fast moving players run into each other, how can you decide whether you're looking at a block or a charge? The question can be answered in a variety of ways.

Let's start with a head-on contact. Your decisions here should be based on the defensive man's guarding position. To be in a legal guarding position, the defender must have his feet planted on the floor, must be stationary, and must be facing his opponent.

The defender may move into the path of a dribbler at any time so long as he has the moment (even split-second) necessary to take a legal stationary position prior to contact. The dribbler then must stop or change direction. If there is contact, the dribbler is guilty of charging.

But suppose the defender comes laterally into the path of the dribbler and makes contact. The chances are that he's guilty of blocking. This is especially true if the dribbler has advanced far enough to get his head and shoulders past the man. Obviously, the defender hasn't had the time to establish a legal stationary position prior to the contact. The call must go against the defender.

A firm restriction, however, applies when the defender moves into the path of a man without the ball. He must take his legal position while his opponent has the distance to stop or change direction. The distance allowable is determined by the speed of the opponent but is never to exceed two steps. If the opponent slams into the defender under these circumstances, the call is charging on the opponent. If the defender mistimes his move and fails to give the offensive man the space in which to stop or change direction, then the call must be for blocking.

On another point the rules read that when opposing players are playing the ball, contact is to be considered incidental if they take due care to avoid each other and, of course, if neither is put at a disadvantage. If there is significant contact while the men are roughly side by side or facing each other, you'll need to judge exactly who bears the greater responsibility for it. But suppose that one is behind the other as they work the ball. The lead man stops. If there is now contact, the blame usually goes to the man at the rear because of his unfavorable position in relation to the ball.

Still another point: There is often contact as a dribbler pivots and drives for the basket. You'll help yourself here by watching the dribbler's feet. If he backs into or turns into a legally positioned defender while making the pivot, the call is charging. But if he takes a step past an oncoming defender (or gets his head and shoulders past him) and is then pressured from the side, it's likely a block.

These very basic examples should help you in making your first blocking and charging calls. In the course of your officiating career, you're going to be looking at a wide variety of such calls. Some contacts will be quite obvious. A great many will be borderline cases, requiring use of personal judgment. In all cases—and especially in the borderline situations—remember that very basic suggestion: Judge who bears the greater responsibility for the contact and make your decision on that basis.

Screening A *screen* is an action taken by one or more players to delay or prevent an opponent from getting to a desired spot on the court. A screen must meet several criteria if it is to be judged legal.

First, there must be no body contact between the screener and the opponent. Second, the screener must not be moving unless he is traveling in exactly the same path and direction as his opponent. Third, during a moving screen, the screener must remain far enough away to permit his man to stop or change direction; when not moving, the screener may be as close to his man as he pleases so long as the man can see him. Finally, when the screen is to the rear of the opponent, the screener must stay at least one step away; since the man being screened can't see to the rear, he must be given the space to back up at least a step without making contact.

With the above information in mind, let's look at several examples of screening plays to see how they should be called.

A defender screens a man who must then go around him to receive a pass from a teammate. The man starts around. There is a very slight contact. The man is unable to take the pass. A foul is called on the screener because by taking the man out of the play he put him at a distinct disadvantage.

Please note that the contact itself was very slight. Though screens to be strictly legal should not involve a contact, you can let slight touches slip past as incidental—but only if they *don't* interfere with the play. Were the screened man in the above example to make the reception, you would ignore the contact and let the game proceed. No one had been harmed.

But take great care in judging how consequential a light contact may actually be. Perhaps more than on any other single play, even the lightest touch on a screen can influence the outcome of the action.

Another example: On a screen from behind, the screener comes well within a step of his man. The man turns and breaks away without contact. The screener is too close to his man but the lack of contact takes precedence. The screened man has not been put at a disadvantage. Forget the call.

In many instances the screener is not the man to be blamed. Suppose that two men establish a legal screen behind a defender. To get to the ball, he turns and tries to muscle his way between them when there is not enough space for passage. Even though he fails to reach his destination, the foul is on him. He's responsible for the unnecessarily hard contact.

Now suppose that some moments later the same men again set up a legal screen behind the same defender. This time he turns and tries to break around them to the right. The screener on that side jumps into his path, too late for the man to stop or change direction. There is contact either from the side or the front. The screener is at fault. The call is against him.

As in all body contact situations, your screening decisions must be based on those often repeated points: Who is more responsible for the contact? Is the opponent put at a disadvantage? In addition, you need always remember that the slightest of contacts on a screen can have a critical influence on the action. Watch closely even for brushes.

Contact with the Shooter Many officials feel that calls for contacts with the shooter are about the most ticklish in the business. These decisions are crucial because a possible score hangs in the balance.

Neither before, during, nor after the goal try may a defender illegally interfere with the shooter and put him at a disadvantage. What is especially difficult to judge here is whether a slight contact, that otherwise would be considered incidental, constitutes enough interference to be called. It's a purely judgmental call on your part. You'll help yourself to a valid judgment by always remembering that, as with the screen, even the slightest of brushes can adversely affect a shot. You might well call contacts here that you'd ignore if made in the same degree against a non-shooter. Also, always be on the lookout to see whether the ball is away or still in the shooter's hand at the time of the light contact. Obviously, the shot is going to be affected only while he's holding the ball or is still in his follow-through.

It's common practice to disregard slight contacts when the goal attempt is successful or when they occur after the goal has been scored. Flagrant contacts, however, must always be called, no matter when they occur.

Slight and transient contacts can be difficult to sight. But you won't miss the more flagrant offenses if you and your fellow official have the play properly surrounded. As a case in point, let's say that as the shooter is jumping for his try, a defender goes up to block the ball, extending one hand high. With his free hand he accidentally or deliberately pushes the shooter with the result that the shot sails off course. From your position, the defender's hand may be screened from view. But if your fellow official is where he's supposed to be—on the other side of the play—he's almost sure to get a good look at the infraction.

Properly positioned and with your eyes open, you should also be able to see those last split-second situations that can qualify as interference. For example, suppose that a defender takes a legal guarding position as the shooter drives in and leaves the floor. But while the shooter is airborne, the defender breaks his position and steps forward, causing the shooter to crash into him on descent. It's a foul on the defender.

Not all contacts, of course, are the fault of the defender, and you must work to protect him as well. Let's say that the defender mentioned above, after taking his legal guarding position, does not move forward as the shooter leaves the floor. Rather, with both arms upraised to block the shot, he rises vertically from the floor. The two men collide. This time the foul goes against the shooter. A defender, once he's assumed the legal position, is entitled to rise through a vertical plane above his body.

So eyes open at all times. Watch for the slightest of contacts. Judge if they adversely affect the shot. Judge who is the responsible party.

Three-Officials System

Certain associations, as was mentioned at the start of the chapter, permit the use of three floor officials. The three-official system provides excellent game coverage and, while presently in limited use, may be *the* system of the future. Steadily growing in popularity, it deserves your attention.

The system employes a referee and two umpires who surround the action by enclosing it within a triangle of observation. Court mechanics call for them to serve on a rotating basis as lead, trail, and center men.

The triangular positioning of the three officials can be easily seen in the stations they take during all front court play. As shown in the illustration, the lead official moves to the end line just as he does in two-official coverage. The trail official works inbounds near the division line on the side of the court adjacent to the scorekeeper's table. The center official handles the opposite side of the court, positioning himself approximately midway between the lead and trail men and shifting his spot as the action dictates.

When the ball changes possession, and the action moves upcourt, the lead official becomes the trail man, while the former trail man takes over the lead; the exchange is the same as in the two-official system. The center official holds onto his job.

At first glance, the mechanics of handling a jump ball may seem complicated; they become simple—even simpler than two-official mechanics—with practice and experience. The center official always administers the toss, facing the scorekeeper's table as he does so. As seen in Figure A, the free officials position themselves about six to ten feet to either side of the tosser and a few feet inbounds from their respective sidelines.

Depending on the direction of the tapped ball, one of the free officials takes over as lead man, and the other becomes either the trail or center man. Figure B shows the change on a ball sent to the tapper's left. The

29.

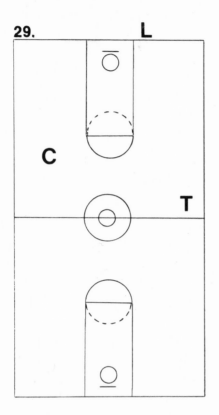

free official on the scorekeeper's side of the court moves to the lead spot. His colleague across the way becomes the center man. And the tosser crosses to the trail position.

If you're working as tosser, a simple formula will tell you where to move after the tap. If the ball heads to your left, as in Figure B, move to the trail spot. If it travels to the right, remain at the center position.

Throw-ins are easy to handle with the triangular coverage. The trail and center men handle throw-ins along the sidelines on their respective sides of the court. The lead official takes the end line throws.

When you run into a foul, the official who calls the infraction always handles the free throw. On the customary exchange of positions after a

30.

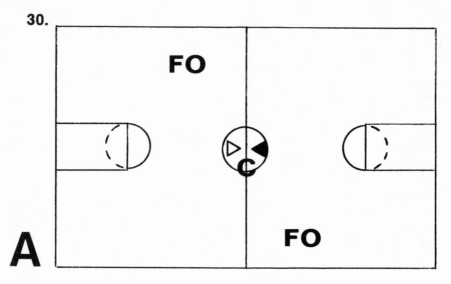

A

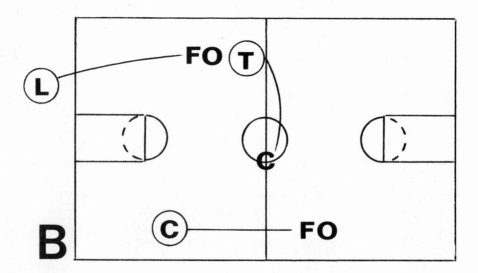

B

foul, he either becomes or remains the center man. His two fellow officials switch jobs.

And that's it—briefly put, the basics of the three-officials system. Of course, there's more to the system than can be covered here. You'll be wise to look closely at the system and acquaint yourself with its mechanics in the coming years. As said earlier, it just may be the system of the future.

Your Uniform

You and your fellow official wear identical uniforms. The uniform consists of a short-sleeve knit shirt and slacks. The slacks are black, and the shirt is vertically striped in black and white. All accessory apparel—belt, socks, shoes, and laces—should be black.

If you wish, you may wear a navy blue jacket before game time and during the intermission period.

The two floor officials should each carry two whistles, the second to be used in the event the first fails. When being used, the whistle should be on a cord that is worn around the neck. It should be equipped with a plastic mouthpiece to give you an easy grip.

Off-court personnel do not wear uniforms. They should, however, be neatly dressed. Slacks and sports jackets are good choices for both men and women. Men will be wise to wear a dress shirt and tie. Neatly dressed, the off-court personnel will have a more "official" appearance that will enhance the game.

6. Tennis

I T   C A N   B E   S A I D   that so far as the number of officials is concerned, tennis is the least superstitious of all sports. It can also be said—and often is—that tennis is the game that uses the greatest number of officials for the least number of players. A full tennis officiating crew consists of thirteen members, its job being to supervise and judge matches being played by two or four competitors.

The Officials

The members of the officiating crew are the *referee,* the *chair umpire,* the *net umpire,* and ten *line umpires.* The line umpires are also known as linesmen. Let's take a look at your duties in each slot.

The Referees Your work as a tennis referee differs from that of the referee in such games as football and soccer. Tennis matches are played as events in a tournament, and ordinarily you do not actually officiate any of the matches. Rather, serving as an ex officio member of the tournament

128

committee, you're charged with the overall supervision of the day's proceedings. You're responsible for seeing that the games progress smoothly—on schedule and in accordance with the rules—and that fairness prevails in the conditions of play.

As for the tournament committee, its primary job is to see that there are proper and adequate facilities for the matches.

You must be on the tourney premises at all times during play, ready to decide on any matters that fall within your jurisdiction. Should you need to leave the grounds, you must appoint a pro tem referee to serve in your place. The same goes if you decide to officiate or participate in one of the matches.

Your overall responsibility divides itself into specifics. First, working independently or in cooperation with the tournament committee, you have the job of scheduling the matches. Then you have the authority to assign the courts and:

• Appoint and remove the various umpires.
• Postpone a match or delay its start because of such factors as rain or darkness. The chair umpire may suspend play on his own due to such problems as poor weather, but only you can actually *postpone* the match.
• Default a player for such reasons as failing to be ready for his match, for misconduct, or for failing to follow your instructions or those of the chair umpire. The chair umpire may also default a player for the above reasons. The player then has the right to appeal the umpire's action. Your decision on the matter is the final one.
• Rule on any question of tennis law that may be referred to you or that the chair umpire may be unable to settle on his own.

You usually work with the tournament chairman to decide on a variety of technical points. For instance, you determine the number of games to be played between ball changes and the number of balls to be allowed per change. You and the chairman also decide whether spikes are to be permitted.

Finally, you're the official who, assisted by one or two committee members, makes the draw prior to the start of play. And you're the official who, if necessary, makes substitutions in the draw.

31.

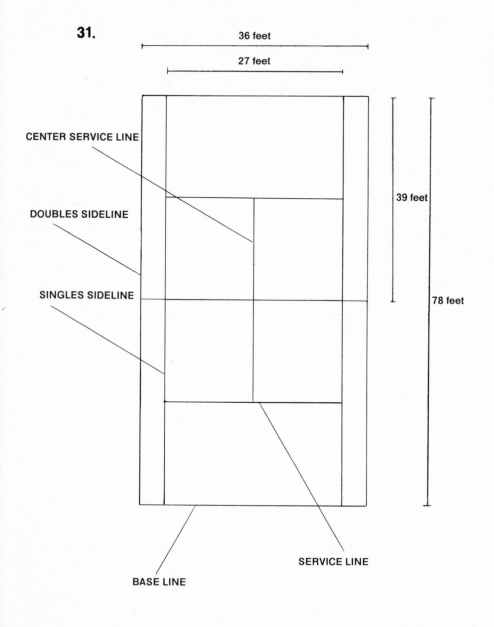

The Chair Umpire As chair umpire, you're the principal official on the court during play. You're charged with the general control of the match assigned to you. Your primary duties call for you to:

- Introduce the match and the players, and announce each player as he serves for the first time.
- Keep a running score of the play, announcing it after point, game, set, and match—and at any time requested by a player.
- Make the calls for which you're responsible and repeat those of your fellow officials that are not clearly voiced or that go unheard because of crowd noise. At one time, it was common practice for the chair umpire to repeat all calls. Now to avoid tiresome repetitions, it's customary for you to echo the calls only when a repeat seems necessary.
- See that the players change ends at the proper times, that the ends are changed within the time specified (usually ninety seconds), and that the players serve and receive in proper rotation.
- Suspend play when circumstances require.
- Control crowd disturbances and behavior.
- Make all decisions needed for the proper conduct of the match.
- Complete your scorecard at the end of the match, sign it, and deliver it to the appropriate authority.

The above listing is intended merely as an introduction to your work. We'll be talking of your duties in greater detail and adding specific assignments to them when we come to the section on the mechanics of officiating.

The Net Umpire You're really the chair umpire's assistant. As such, your primary jobs are to:

- Keep a duplicate scorecard as a double check on the chair umpire.
- Measure—or help the chair umpire to measure—the height of the net prior to the match and at the changeover games that mark the start of each set. You're also to measure the net at any time the chair deems it necessary or advisable.
- Put the singles sticks in place—or remove them if there's no need for them.
- Call or signal "net" to make sure that the chair is aware that a served ball has touched the net.

32.

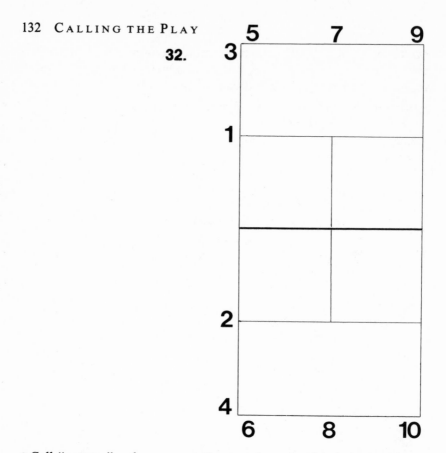

- Call "not-ups" unless requested not to do so by the chair. Under certain systems of play only the chair umpire may make "not-up" calls, while under others the job is left to you unless he wants it for himself. You and the chair should agree beforehand on who is to take the calls. The man selected should then be the *only* one responsible for them.
- Assist the chair umpire in keeping track of ball changes and in instructing and supervising the ball boys.

Line Umpire You and your fellow line umpires—or linesmen—are stationed in chairs around the perimeter of the court. The chairs are placed as far back from the court boundaries as possible so that you never interfere with the players. The distribution of the linesmen is shown in illustration 32. Each position is designated by a number. When you're given your assignment, it will be by one of the numbers so that there will be no confusion over the location of your station.

On taking your station, you're charged with a single task. You watch the court line assigned to you and judge whether any ball falling near that line is out or playable. Your calls are two—"out" and "fault." (The latter call is not to be confused with "foot fault," but refers to any served ball that clears the net but falls outside any of the service box lines.) You're to make no calls for lines other than your own. And with one exception you're to limit yourself to the "out" and "fault" calls.

The exception: If you're assigned to a baseline (positions 3 and 4), you'll be additionally responsible for calling foot faults. The job of calling foot faults will also come your way occasionally when you work the sidelines or the center service lines (positions 7 and 8).

The Mechanics of Officiating

Like their colleagues in other sports, tennis officials over the years have developed a series of procedures and techniques for attending to their duties in the most effective way possible. In this section, we'll look closely at how best to handle the many specific tasks which are your primary responsibilities when a match is played.

The Chair Umpire at Work Your work begins the moment you pick up your scorecard prior to the match. Immediately check on all the details that must be known about the match. Your checklist should include: (1) the name of the tournament, (2) division—men, women, singles, doubles, etc., (3) round, (4) best of?, (5) ball change, (6) type of scoring, (7) point penalties in effect, and (8) names and residences of the players. Depending on the nature of the tourney, *residence* here means the player's school, association, city, county, or state.

All the above information is vital to your supervision of the match. Actually, the tournament officials should have it listed on the card and ready for you at the time of your arrival. But sometimes there are slip-ups. So take the time to check the card thoroughly. If any point is missing, obtain the needed information before you head for the court.

Also, make sure that you're carrying at least two pencils. Both should have erasers. It's a good idea to bring along a small pencil sharpener—just in case it's needed.

If at all possible, you should arrive at the court with or ahead of the players. On meeting them for the first time, take extra care to learn the correct pronunciations of their names. You'll be announcing the names throughout the match, and if there's anything that can upset a player (not to mention his fans), it's the torture of hearing his name continually mispronounced. Names that are tongue-twisters or call for odd pronunciations can lead to some embarrassing stumbles along the way if you don't take care of things here.

On arrival at the court immediately join the net umpire for a check of the net height, measuring it at the posts and the center service line and then adjusting it if necessary. See that the net man sets the singles sticks in place or, as the case may be, removes them. Finally, check to see that there is an adequate supply of balls and that your viewing platform is equipped with any extra equipment that you may want or need. The platform, standing about five-feet high, should be centered on an imaginary line extending out from the net and should be placed several feet distant from the net post.

Take a moment now to consult with the net umpire on how the two of you will divide the calls that ordinarily fall within your province. As has been remarked, the net umpire is to call "not ups" unless you otherwise request. You'll also need to decide who is to handle the calls when (1) a player volleys or smashes the ball before it comes into his court, (2) a player or anything he is wearing or carrying (exclusive of his racket when making a stroke) touches the ball while it is in play, (3) a player enters his opponent's court, or (4) the ball touches an overhead fixture or goes through the net.

A clear understanding of who is to handle these calls will avoid the problem of both of you talking at once during the match. Though you may divide the calls as you wish, it is general practice to reserve illegal stroke decisions for yourself.

Now it's time to check the line umpires. See that they're positioned as assigned by the tournament. You may run into a problem here. So many linesmen are needed in a tourney (for example, forty if four matches are played simultaneously) that there may not be enough to go around. If you're not blessed with a full complement, position the linesmen in the spots where you think they'll give the best coverage. Placement will depend on such factors as the nature of the match and the type of court. In general, though, think of those stations that are most difficult for you to see from your platform—the base, side, and service lines farthest from you. If you wish, you may shift the net umpire to a linesman's spot and handle all the umpiring chores by yourself.

If there are ball boys, make certain they understand the players' preferences for the clearing of balls on missed first serves. Instruct them to move all balls quickly to the server's end when there is a change of court.

Now you come to your final pregame duty. Supervise the toss of the coin or spin of the racket to decide choice of service or court, then prepare your scorecard for the first set. If necessary, allow the players a brief warm-up period and warn them at the two- and one-minute marks before game time. Check that your fellow officials are ready to work. Start the match at its scheduled time.

The match begins with your opening announcement in which the players are introduced and the first server named. Throughout the game, you'll be responsible for a number of announcements. Before talking about them in turn, let's consider some general points.

The announcements, of course, are all-important to the game. They keep the spectators and players informed on the progress of play, and when properly made, they contribute mightily to fashioning a smoothly played game. They're also important to you. They give the most visible sign of your skills as an umpire. If they're well made, you look good. But if they're halting, confused, or inaudible, you suffer. Everyone focuses on the obvious shortcoming and begins to doubt your overall abilities. You can end up with an annoyed crowd—and, worse, two or four nervous players—on your hands.

The five suggestions that follow should help get your announcements off to a good start. Chair umpires have taken advantage of them for years.

- Make all announcements clearly in an unhurried and confident voice. Announcements that go unheard are obviously useless. Hurried announcements can convey a sense of upset or nervousness that can quickly disconcert the players. And, of course, hurried announcements leave you especially vulnerable to error.

- Time the announcements so that the largest audience is available for them. Time and again there will be applause at the moment when an announcement must be made—for instance, after a point is scored. Don't hurry yourself. Wait until the applause dies down. Then speak.
- If you make an error or announce a linesman's decision that he then reverses, don't become flustered. Take a moment to arrange your thoughts. Then make the revised announcement—clearly and slowly, please.
- There will be times when, for the welfare of the players and the smooth conduct of the match, you must ask for quiet from the spectators. Do so in a courteous and friendly, but dignified, manner. Never let an angry edge creep into your voice. It's also important to know *when* to ask for quiet. You have to use your own judgment here, but, in general, you should never allow excessive spectator movement, unruly behavior, or heavy applause to continue for what you consider too long a time. Always remember how quickly any of these activities can upset the players.
- Make all announcements in a friendly and objective manner, never letting a player feel that you disapprove of his play or that you favor, even in the slightest, his opponent. Jack Stahr of the United States Tennis Association calls any tennis official "a friend at court." It's an apt and concise description of your position in a match. Let your voice live up to the description.

Now for the announcements themselves. They number six. You'll announce (1) the start of the match, (2) each player as he serves for the first time, (3) each point scored, (4) point after deuce, (5) game and set winners, and (6) match and winner.

The rules of tennis themselves do not prescribe the exact way in which the announcements should be worded. But a set procedure for making each announcement has been developed over the years and has become traditional. It's designed to provide all the needed information in a clear and given order.

Start of the Match: The announcement contains, in turn, the name of the tournament, the names of the players and their residences, the nature of the match, and the name of the first server. The following example should serve you well.

"Ladies and gentlemen. This is a first round match in the City Inter-scholastic Clay Court Tournament, men's singles. On my right is Mr. John Thomas of Central High School. On my left, Mr. Harold Grayson of Suburban High School. This will be the first of three sets. Mr. Thomas won the toss and has elected to serve."

Once the announcement is made, glance at your fellow officials and ask, "Linesmen ready?" On seeing their nods, pause a moment and then open the match with the simple instruction, "Play!"

First Serves: On all subsequent first serves, the announcement is simply "Mr. Thomas (or Mr. Grayson) to serve." You should use the formal titles *Mr., Mrs., Miss,* or *Ms.* on the first of these announcements, but you're free to drop them thereafter. The trend nowadays is to dispense with them in the interests of being brief and avoiding repetition.

Each Point Scored: The basic rule is to announce the server's score first. If the server wins the first two points, the announcements are: "15-love" and "30-love." Should the receiver win the third point, the announcement is "30-15."

Point after Deuce: The point that breaks a deuce (a tie at three-all or at any time thereafter) is simply announced "Advantage, Mr. Thomas." As in the case of points scored, the current trend is to drop the formal title, making the announcement "Advantage, Thomas." Often in long deuce games the advantage is announced so frequently that the formal title becomes tiresomely repetitious.

The calling of advantages in doubles matches can be awkward if you attempt to use the names of both players. It's customary simply to announce the server's name.

Game Score: The announcement at the end of a game begins with the winner's name—"Game, Mr. Thomas" or "Game, Thomas." The score also should be given so that the entire announcement becomes: "Game, Thomas. Games are two-one, first set. Thomas leads."

Set Score: When a game determines the winner of a set, your announcement is "Game and first set, (Mr.) Thomas, six-four." After the first set, the set score should be announced periodically, say after every three or four games. Take care to avoid announcing the set scores too often; it's a practice that can easily upset the trailing player. An example of your announcement: "Games are four-three. Mr. Grayson leads, third set. (Mr.) Thomas won the first two sets."

Match and Winner: At the end of the match, announce: "Game, set, and match, (Mr.) Thomas." Then announce the set scores. The match winner's scores are always announced first.

Now for a final three points about your announcements. First, always mark the score on your card before announcing it; it's a practice that will reduce the possibility of announcing errors. Second, if you discover that you've made an error in the score, immediately correct it and announce the correction. Finally, announce points only *after* they've been scored; never announce that an upcoming point is a set or a match point; while you may think you're adding a degree of excitement to the proceedings, you'll likely succeed only in disconcerting the players.

The Linesman at Work As you know, your job is to decide whether balls falling near your line are good or out. The job, it's true, is a simple one. But there's an element of danger in its simplicity. If you're not careful, your mind can wander or your eye can be distracted by some off-court occurrence.

Your basic technique, then, must be to keep your attention focused on the court at all times, constantly ready for the ball to arrive in your area. Many of your calls will be close ones. As any experienced linesman will tell you, the laws of fate being what they are, a close one is sure to come your way at the very moment your attention strays.

Your sense of timing is vital, when watching for outs. As the ball heads into your area, you must locate its landing spot prior to its arrival. Otherwise, if you attempt to follow the ball in, your vision may blur. Pick the approximate spot where the ball seems destined to land. Settle your gaze there. You'll focus on the ball if it lands anywhere in that area.

While you must anticipate the ball's arrival, don't allow yourself to make a premature call. Wait until the ball actually strikes. Then if it's out, make the call, simultaneously signaling the chair umpire with an upraised arm. Make the call in a strong, clear voice so there will be no need for the chair to bother with a repeat. To stress a point made several times earlier, repetitions tire the spectators and the players. Continue holding your arm upraised until the chair sees you.

Every "out" must be called aloud, even when the ball obviously sails out of the playing area before touching the ground. The same goes for "faults." When you say nothing, it means just one thing: the ball is good.

As carefully as you may work, you're bound to make an error at one time or another. The chances are that you'll prematurely raise your arm on a ball that turns out to be good. Don't let the mistake rattle you. Immediately get the chair umpire's attention and indicate the correction. Likewise, get his attention right away if he fails to hear your call correctly and makes an announcement not in keeping with your decision.

There will also be times when you can't reach a decision on a ball falling near your line. Either call the chair or signal him by placing both hands over your eyes. He'll seek the assistance of another umpire who has perhaps seen the play and will then attempt to make a proper judgment.

Though watching your own line attentively, always try to be alert to the areas near you. Your opinion may be needed on a call there. You should give your opinion only when requested to do so; never volunteer; an unsolicited opinion is considered an intrusion. And, of course, you should give an opinion only if you're positive that it's the correct one. No guessing.

Courtesy is the hallmark of any tennis official and especially of the linesman. Courtesy requires that you sit quietly at your station and do your job. During play, you should avoid shifting in your chair and should never stand and walk about. Nor should you ever smoke. And, above all, never strike up a conversation with a fellow linesman or begin to comment on the game. The players are close by, well within hearing distance, and you must not be responsible for a remark that upsets or distracts them.

Scoring

In scorekeeping tennis differs from many other sports. There is not a separate scorekeeper. The chair umpire keeps score, and the net umpire maintains an additional scorecard as a double-check.

Tennis is not a difficult game to score. Once you're acquainted with the scorecard and have begun to fill it in prior to the game, you should have no difficulty.

In the illustration the column at the left (A) is numbered with the games in the set. Column B is set aside for the initials of the servers. After the coin toss or spin of the racket has decided the first server, you should fill in the column with the initials, alternating them as shown.

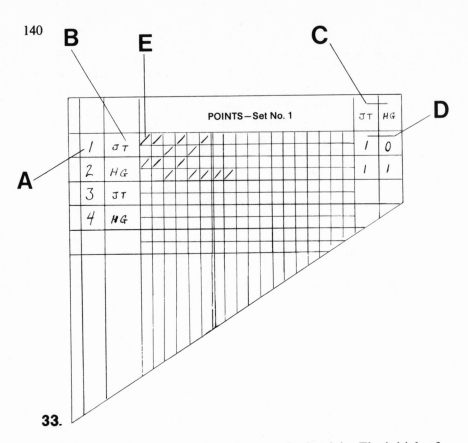

33.

Let's skip across the card to the column at the far right. The initials of the servers are placed in the columns marked C; the game results belong in those marked D. The actual scores are not listed in columns D, but only notations of who won and who lost the game. In the example, Thomas won the first game, making the score 1-0, after which Grayson went on to tie things at 1-1.

Now for the boxes (E) stretching across the face of the card. There are two sets of boxes, one above the other, alongside each server's initials. The points tallied are placed in these boxes as the game progresses. The server's tallies go into the upper set while the receiver's tallies are placed in the lower set. In the opening game, the server won the first point, making the score 15-love. He won again for 30-love. The receiver then won a point: 30-15. The server: 40-15. The receiver: 40-30. The server: game.

In the second game, the score reads: 15-love, 30-love, 30-15, 40-15, 40-30, deuce, advantage G, and game G.

Your Uniform

There is no mandatory uniform for tennis officials. All clothing worn by officials should, of course, be neat, clean, and somewhat on the formal side to help set a businesslike atmosphere for the matches.

Though white is the traditional playing garb in tennis, it is inappropriate for the linesmen. It creates a difficult background against which to play. Linesmen should wear dark clothing to help them blend into the background.

7. Track and Field

TENNIS MAY WELL BOAST the greatest number of officials for the fewest players. But by actual count the officiating crew at a track and field meet has to be the largest in sports. Depending on the size of a meet, the crew can range from twenty-five to more than 150 people.

The Officials

Basically there are twelve officiating positions on a track and field crew. The crew size balloons in relation to the meet size because of the number of assistants that several of the officials then must have. The officials are:

1. The *referee*
2. The *clerk of the course* and, if necessary, assistants
3. The *starter* and, optionally, a recall (assistant) starter
4. The *head finish judge* and assistants
5. The *head timer,* three assistant timers, a substitute timer, and—if placements after the winner are to be timed—additional assistants

6. The *head inspector* and assistants
7. The *head field judge*
8. *Event judges* for each field event
9. The *scorer*
10. The *marshal* and, if necessary, assistants
11. The *meet announcer*
12. The *wind gauge operator.*

Track and field meets are planned and presented by a games committee headed by the meet director. On attending your first meet, you'll find that additional personnel, though not actually a part of the officiating crew, is needed to make the day run smoothly. On hand, for instance, should be a press steward who provides sports reporters with information concerning the meet itself and the results of the various competitions. A custodian of awards will be there to care for and present the trophies and medals to the winners. A physician is needed to attend to any medical emergencies.

The Referee Should you work as referee, your duties will be somewhat similar to those of the tennis referee. Your basic responsibility does not call for you to judge any of the events. Rather, your function is to see that the meet is conducted in accordance with the rules. When there are questions concerning infractions, you're the official who answers them and settles any disputes or misunderstandings. Yours is the final word on the interpretation of the rules. If there is disagreement with your decision, the competitor or coach involved may later appeal to the games committee or to an appeals committee established for the meet.

In addition to your basic responsibility, you have several specific duties. You're the official who must:

• Check and certify the performances that break records in any of the events.
• Suspend the meet due to such emergencies as poor weather conditions or unruly crowd behavior.
• Alter the order of competition in the events if circumstances warrant, with the approval of the games committee.

You're also authorized to disqualify contestants for unsportsmanlike conduct and unacceptable behavior. In the rules published by the National Federation of State High School Associations, unsportsmanlike conduct is defined as conduct which is unethical or dishonorable, including such acts as using profanity, criticizing a fellow competitor, or treating an official with disrespect. The guilty contestant can be barred from the meet for the rest of the day. Unacceptable behavior covers such acts as impeding fellow competitors and willfully failing to follow an official's instructions; the penalty is disqualification from the event in which the conduct is observed.

Additionally, you're charged with at least two premeet duties. You're to:

- See that the track and field are properly marked.
- Make certain that all equipment is in place and that its condition is up to standard. Most meets have a *hurdle chief*. He and his assistants—called the hurdle crew—are responsible for putting the hurdles in place just before they're used and then later removing them. He alone often needs from ten to twenty assistants. If possible, you should check their work.

You may also need to do some "doubling in brass." Most meets of any size have a *head of officials,* whose job is to supervise the officiating crew. In smaller meets, however, you may be asked to handle his job as well as yours. If so, your premeet duties will also include:

- Assigning your fellow officials to their events.
- Conferring with the officials to review their duties. Because of the large crew needed, meets must often depend on inexperienced help to one degree or another. You may be forced to use beginners not only as assistants but as head officials as well. You and the starter, singly or together, should coach them in their duties.

If you're involved in a championship meet, you'll be expected as referee to hold a premeet conference with the starter, the coaches, and perhaps the team captains. The time should be used to review the various procedures that will be followed, to answer questions, and to explain any special instructions that you may have.

Some final points: In dual meets the job of referee often goes to the host coach or athletic director. You and the starter should be the most experienced men on the crew. In smaller meets, the referee may be asked to serve as starter as well.

Now let's turn to the other crew members and put you at their spots. You'll find them divided into three groups. One group handles the track events while the other takes care of the field work. The third group provides the meet with what can be called general services.

The Officials: Track Events

The following officials and their assistants are responsible for the track events: (1) the clerk of the course, (2) the starter, (3) the head finish judge, (4) the head timer, and (5) the head inspector.

The Clerk of the Course In the eyes of many an official, yours is the most demanding job at the meet. Armed with a list of the events and their entrants, you must see that the day progresses on schedule by having all the competitors in the right place and ready to race at the right time.

The Starter Though the clerk of the course has the most demanding job in its detail, you're regarded as the single most important track official. Once the runners are ready for a race, they're in your charge. It's your duty to start them down the track, to see that the start is clean and legal, and to recall them for a new try if there is a false start.

The Head Finish Judge Watching the runners cross the finish line, you and your assistants determine the winner and the subsequent placements. It's ticklish work because the runners are often closely bunched as they flash across the line.

The Head Timer To you and your assistants goes the job of recording the winning time posted in each race. You may also be asked by the games committee to time other placements.

The Head Inspector You're responsible for observing the races to see that they're run without lane violations. In particular you watch to see that the runners neither change direction nor impede their opponents. Relay races call for you to determine whether the baton is passed in the prescribed passing zone. Ideally, you work with three assistants. The four of you are stationed at points along the track.

The Officials: Field Events

The field events are officiated by the head field judge and the event judges.

The Head Field Judge As your title implies, you supervise the overall conduct of the field events and the work of the judges assigned to them. If the meet is for teenagers, the maximum number of events in your charge will likely be seven—the pole vault, high jump, long jump, triple jump, discus, shot put, and javelin.

The Event Judges You and your fellow judges see that the event to which you're assigned is conducted in accordance with the rules. One of your number is always designated the *chief event judge*. He rules on the performance of each contestant while the rest of the crew marks and measures the throws or jumps. He's also charged with seeing that the crew works quickly and accurately.

The Officials: General Services

The officials who provide general services are (1) the scorer, (2) the marshal, (3) the meet announcer, and (4) the wind gauge operator.

The Scorer Yours is the job of maintaining a running record of the team scores as the results of the various events are reported to you. Your scoring account should also contain a record of individual winners and their performances.

The Marshal You and your assistants are charged with keeping all the competitive areas clear so that no one impedes the progress of any event. Unless otherwise authorized, spectators and athletes not competing in the event in progress are to remain away from the track and the infield. Your aim is to see that the meet progresses steadily and smoothly.

The Meet Announcer Stationed at a public address microphone, you introduce each event and the competitors and then announce the results as soon as they're made available to you. Additionally, you provide general information for the convenience of the spectators (locations of restrooms, drinking fountains, refreshment stands, exits, etc.) and, if necessary, assist the marshal by requesting the spectators and the athletes to help maintain an atmosphere conducive to the success of the meet. At the close of the day you introduce the winners as they receive their awards and announce the final scores and team standings.

The Wind Gauge Operator An anomometer is needed to determine wind direction and velocity so that their effects can be calculated when validating certain performances. As its operator, you'll be called on to take wind readings during the long and triple jumps and during races up to and including 200 meters. The readings are reported to the scorer and made a part of the permanent meet record.

The Mechanics of Officiating: Track Events

Certain of the track officials must employ specific procedures and techniques to get their work successfully done. Continuing the tactic of moving you from one post to another, let's look at these mechanics of officiating.

The Clerk of the Course at Work Your basic work tool is the roster of the events and their competitors. It may be developed by the games committee and handed to you before or on meet day. Or the committee may ask you to take on the job of developing it. (You may also be asked to compile the roster of field events). If so, it will be your responsibility to assign the runners to their heats. The assignments are usually made according to the runners' past performances. All necessary information should come from the competing schools, either directly or via the games committee. A few telephone calls to the schools may be required to tie down all the details.

On arriving at the meet site, you should immediately be in touch with the competitors so that you can:

- Inform them of the rules governing the day's events. This information should include the methods planned for qualifying for the semifinal and final heats. The runners should also be told of the number of placements to be scored in each race.
- Assign each runner to his heat and starting position if these assignments have not already been made by the games committee.
- Remind the competitors that, when they go out to the track, they must be properly uniformed and wearing their assigned numbers. The members of relay teams must wear uniforms of the same color.

The lane assignments in each race are usually decided by the drawing of lots (depending on the wishes of the games committee, even the heats themselves may be decided in this manner). You may be asked to conduct the drawing, recording the assignments on your roster as you go along. Folded slips of paper with the lane numbers on them may be used. A common and more convenient practice—it saves the time of refolding the papers for each new drawing—is to use blank cartridges that have the lane numbers printed on their ends.

As the day progresses, you'll also have to conduct the drawings for the heat and lane assignments in the semifinal and final races.

Once the races begin, your duties mount. Immediately prior to each race, you must:

- Assemble the runners at the starting line in time for the event, give them any final instructions that may be needed, and see that each takes his assigned lane.
- Distribute the batons if the race is a relay. You're to collect them at the end of the event.
- Rearrange the lane assignments if necessary. Perhaps you find that a lane—or a section of it—is damaged and may not be used. Perhaps not all the assigned runners have appeared for the event.
- See that the head finish judge receives a card containing the runners' names, numbers, and lane assignments.
- Turn the runners over to the starter when all is in readiness.

While these jobs are assigned to you by the rules, they may be shared with the recall starter. Further, the games committee, if it wishes, may assign them all to him so you're left free for your other duties.

There's little doubt that you're going to need several assistants, especially if faced with a meet of substantial size. You should arrange your assistants so that one is attending to the runners in the current race while another is holding the group for the next race in readiness.

Possibly your most demanding assignment is to keep the meet on schedule. Do all that you can to have the races start at their scheduled times—or as soon thereafter as possible. Remember, however, that no race should start before its scheduled time.

Finally, in the midst of all else, don't forget the meet announcer. Keep him provided with up-to-date information on the races so that his announcements will always be complete and accurate.

The Starter at Work Depending on the amount of help that can be mustered for the day, you may work alone or with a recall starter (in some associations, he's called an assistant starter). If alone, you're responsible not only for launching each race but also for judging false starts (premature moves across the starting line). If one occurs, you're to recall the runners for a new try. Should you have a recall starter, he'll handle the false-start problem and signal the recalls. He'll also be responsible for recalls when a runner, not through his own fault, takes a tumble on the first turn.

Two starting guns are to be used—one for the start itself and one for the recall. Both—and especially the starting gun itself—should be the type that can be cocked for instant firing. The recall gun can be a .22 caliber, but your best choice for the starting gun is a .32 caliber because it flashes more strongly. The flash, traveling faster than the sound of the gunshot, serves as the signal to the distant finish judges and timers that the race has started. Blank cartridges filled with black powder should be used.

Immediately prior to each race, you and the assistant should check the guns to see that they're continuing to work properly. As soon as the runners assemble at the starting line, direct all attendants and non-competitors to move well away from the track; have all talk and movement stop so that the runners can concentrate fully on you and the coming event. While they're still in their warmup suits, give them their final instructions, telling them to respond quickly and smoothly to your starting commands. Let them know that you'll allow them adequate time to take their starting positions and set themselves. Ask if they have any questions.

Your handling of the youngsters at this time is all-important. They're nervous and keyed to a high pitch. Speak to them in a friendly fashion and with that quiet authority that is invariably calming. Allow nothing to happen on or off the track that will distract or upset them; if, by chance, there's some unsettling incident, take an extra moment to let everything return to normal. Always remember that your attitude and your control of the situation are vital safeguards against false or late starts.

Once the preliminaries are out of the way, have the runners remove their warmup suits. Sound your whistle to let the finish judges and timers know that the race is about to begin; the head finish judge will whistle in return as a signal that his people are ready. Now settle your full attention on the runners.

With the starting gun cocked and raised overhead, give the command, "On your marks." Allow the runners sufficient time to position themselves so that they're comfortable and motionless. Now comes the command, "Set." Watch that all immediately assume the final set position. When all are set *and* motionless, with no one thrusting forward towards a head start, fire the gun.

It is vital to watch the runners' timing to insure a start that will be fair to all. So that no one is made to wait and tense up, the runners must react immediately to both commands. If there's a late or slow response to either, call the proceedings off, have everyone stand and relax, warn the offender not to delay again, and start over. On giving the "set" order, it's best to wait no more than one or two seconds before firing the gun. That's enough time for the runners to settle in but not enough to give them the fidgets.

Now let's look at the exact spot where you work. It will depend on whether the race is being launched from a straight-line or staggered start. For the straight-line start, you and your assistant should be stationed on either side of the track. Your assistant should be directly alongside the starting line and about three to five yards off the track itself; he must be there to watch the runners' hands and feet for false starts. You may position yourself wherever you feel most comfortable, either alongside or to the front or rear of the competitors. A position five to eight yards in front of the runners and perhaps a yard off the track is recommended. If you're working by yourself, of course, you'll need to position yourself so that you can easily see the runners' hands and feet.

When the race is launched from a staggered start as it will be if the runners are to circle the track, you'll need to stand in front of the starting line for a reason we'll see in a moment. Several positions are available to you. If there are, for instance, seven or eight contestants, you may stand on the track itself at some point that is roughly equidistant from all the runners; you may also choose to station yourself off the track just ahead of the outside lane. For a four-man start, take a position on or off the track that is an equal distance from everyone. If you're on the track itself, remain close enough to the edge so that you can step clear before the runners sweep past.

On staggered starts of more than four runners, the recall starter stands off the track alongside the runner on the inside lane. When there are just four runners, his station is just beyond the outside lane. From either position, he sights along the runners at an angle to see their hands and feet.

You must stand to the front of the line on staggered starts because it is necessary for the runners to have you in view. Staggered starts put you at a distance that may be a shade too great for your voice commands to be readily heard by some of the runners. So you may need to bring a combination of hand and whistle signals into play.

Start with five or six short blasts on the whistle; this tells the runners to stand at their marks and signals the finish line people that the race is at hand. On hearing the head finish judge's return whistle, raise the starting gun, sound one long blast on the whistle, swing your free arm backwards and up overhead, and then bring it down so that you're pointing at the ground; its descent is the "on your marks" signal. The "set" signal is another single blast on the whistle and an upward swing that brings the arm straight overhead. Fire when the runners are set and motionless. You may cancel things at any time by hitting the whistle for several short blasts and bringing your arm down in front of your body.

When working a straight-line start, you may also need to bolster your voice commands with the above arm signals. It's often necessary to do so when the stadium noise is especially heavy.

In addition to your duties during the races, a number of premeet tasks fall within your bailiwick. Always be sure to:

• Inspect and test the starting and recall guns. Make sure that you have sufficient cartridges to last the day.

- Inspect the starting and finishing lines, the relay staggers, the exchange zones, and the cut-in flags. Everything should be up to standard and in proper condition for the coming events.
- Talk with the head finish judge to make certain that you both understand the procedures to be followed during the meet.
- Meet with the clerk of the course regarding the instructions that the two of you will give the runners at the starting line. The idea is to avoid bothering the runners with duplicate instructions.

The Head Finish Judge at Work As you know, you and your assistants watch the finish line and determine the order of placements in each race. Depending on the type of meet being held and the number of placements to be judged, your crew can be a sizable one. The responsibility for judging the given placements is divided among the assistants. In dual meets you can get by with one assistant per placement. But in championship affairs you'll need at least two assistants per placement.

You work as both supervisor and judge. As supervisor, you see to it that the assistants are properly stationed at the finish line, each with instructions on how he must cover his placement. As judge, you take a position that gives you an overall view of the finish line. You then note your own opinion of the placements so that you can serve as the final arbiter on any disagreements among the assistants.

And there will be disagreements in the course of the day. It's usually easy—at least, reasonably easy—to identify the winner of a race. But the pursuing runners can be so closely bunched together that their exact order of finish becomes almost impossible to determine with absolute certainty. In a moment, we'll look at what you must do to straighten things out and put the placements into an official order.

But first, assuming that you're working a championship meet with two assistants per placement, let's talk about your supervisory duties. Things start when you assign the assistants to their placements and equip them with pencils and pads of paper supplied by the games committee. The assistants for each placement are to be stationed on either side of the finish line. If the meet grounds are well equipped, there will be staircaselike risers to either side of the line. The assistants arrange themselves on the steps so that each can see the line above the head of the man in front of him.

Should there be a beginner on your crew, you'll need to coach him in his job. Instruct him that, to save time afterwards, he's to write the name of the event and his place assignment on one of the slips of paper prior to the start of a race. Once the race is on, he may watch the runners as they approach. But when they're within ten or fifteen yards of the tape, he must focus on the finish line and hold his gaze there. As the runners sweep across the line (they're "home" once any part of the torso crosses the line), he's to concentrate on his placement only, marking his paper with the number of the runner who crosses in that spot. When making his notation, he's to work completely on his own so that his decision will be unbiased. He's not to ask the opinion of a fellow judge. Nor, as a check against his own, is he to look at the numbers being noted around him. And he must not glance across the track for some indication of what his placement partner has noted.

Three tips should be of particular help to him. First, though excited by the race, he must never give in to the natural tendency to follow the lead runner as the man crosses the line; all his concentration must remain on the line and his assigned placement. Second—and this is an art even more difficult to master—he must not allow himself to look at a runner who falls while approaching the line. Finally, even if he's uncertain about his choice, he should still mark it down immediately. Warn him not to attempt to reconstruct the finish in his mind's eye. Even within a few seconds, his memory will begin to mislead him. He's wisest if he goes with his instinctive choice.

Now for your own judging duties. Watch the race from a spot that gives you a good overall view of the finish; the top step on one of the risers is an obvious choice here. Note *all* the placements as you see them. Once the race is over, collect the slips of paper from your assistants. And here, on three counts at least, is where you're apt to run into difficulty. For openers, you may find that two of the partners don't agree on their placement. Call them to one side and see if the three of you can come to a common agreement. If a single choice doesn't emerge, you must make the final decision yourself. You may have to decide on the basis of your own notations. You may be helped by finding that one assistant's selection agrees with yours.

Next, on looking at all the slips of paper, you may find that one runner has been awarded more than one placement. This matter is solved by assigning him to the highest of the placements noted for him.

Finally, there's going to come the time when you definitely see a runner cross in one of the placement spots only to find that all the assistants have somehow overlooked him. This is a particular danger in very tightly bunched finishes. You're authorized to disregard the notations and assign him to the place in which you saw him finish.

Once the order of finish, whether questioned or not, has been determined, you must fill in your record card, sign it, and deliver it to the scorer.

In addition to the above duties, you're also responsible for the answering whistle that lets the starter know your people are ready for the race. It's suggested that you always arrive at the meet site at least forty-five minutes before the first race. You'll need the time to meet with the referee for any instructions he may have, to collect the necessary papers and pencils for your assistants, and to meet, coach, and assign your crewmen to their stations.

The Head Timer at Work Under ordinary circumstances, you work with three assistant timers and a substitute timer. When blessed with a full crew, you need not actually do any timing yourself, but smaller meets will likely see you holding a watch and serving as one of the assistant timers. At the end of each race the watches held by the three assistant timers are checked to determine the winning time. The substitute timer's watch comes into play only when an assistant runs into trouble and fails to get a complete or accurate reading.

Your quartet, as indicated above, records the winning time only. If subsequent placements are to be timed, each will require its own crew. Ideally, each crew should number four. The officials in your charge, then, can easily outnumber those under the wing of the head finish judge.

Here's how each of your crews should work. On being assigned their individual placement, their station is at the finish line with two men on each side of the track. If they join the finish judges on the risers, they should take the lowest steps possible so that they can sight right along the tape. Once they're in place, have them trigger their watches before each race to see that they're continuing to operate properly. Then on hearing the starter's warning whistle, give the command "Timers, check your watches"; this is not an instruction to determine working order but to double-check that the sweep hands are properly set. Next, when you see the starter raise his arm, call "Gun up"; all attention must now focus on the starting line. The watches are triggered in the instant of the starting gun's flash. If the start proves to be a false one, order the watches stopped and the sweep hands reset.

Before going further, we need to look at two techniques for handling the watches with maximum efficiency. First, each timer should be instructed not to trigger his watch by depressing the stem with his thumb. Rather, have him hold the watch so that the stem is depressed with the forefinger. Studies show that the forefinger reacts a critical shade faster than the thumb.

Second, coach him not merely to hold the watch in readiness when he hears your "gun up" call. Rather, to insure an instant start, he's to depress the stem to the point where all slack ends and then hold it steadily there. On the gun, it's depressed the rest of the way.

Your timers work in much the same way as the finish judges. They may watch the approaching runners. But when the competitors are ten to fifteen yards from the tape, all eyes go to the finish line and sight along it. In the instant that any part of the lead (or assigned placement) runner's torso reaches the line, the watches are to be stopped.

Like the finish judges, your timers should be coached not to be distracted by any action near the tape, especially that of a runner taking a tumble. In addition, to be certain that the watches are instantly stopped, coach them to depress the stems to the end of the slack as the runners enter their final yards.

The forefinger should be used to stop as well as start the watches—and for the same reason. Explain that the watches should be started and stopped with as litle extraneous action as possible. Many timers, especially on the stop, join the finger movement with a jerk or swing of the arm, as if for emphasis. That swing can delay the stop (or start) by a vital fraction of a second.

As soon as the race ends, each timer checks his watch and marks its reading on a slip of paper. Again, he works just as the finish judges do. His notation is made without consulting his companions and without glancing at their figures. The papers then come to you for the computation of the official time for each placement. Be sure to warn each timer not to snap the sweep hand back to its starting point until you've checked his notation and have given him permission to do so.

With luck the readings for any given placement are going to be the same. But the likelihood is that, because the watches are customarily calibrated in tenths of a second, the readings will differ slightly. In the event that the three readings are all different, the middle one becomes the official time. When two readings have an identical time, it's the official one.

Your work for the race ends when you post the official time on your record card, sign the card, and send it to the scorer. Then you're to organize your crew for the next event. In case the winning runner has posted a record performance, be sure to have the referee verify the time by checking the watches.

Along with the head finish judge, you should arrive at least forty-five minutes before the meet. Your pregame jobs take time and include:

- Securing the watches from the games committee and checking their working order. It's also your job to return the watches at day's end.
- Securing and distributing to your crew the paper and pencils needed for their notations.
- Coaching the timers in their duties and rehearsing them in the use of the watches.
- Appointing the timers who will serve as assistants and those who will work as substitutes.
- Assigning the timers to their placements and to their positions on either side of the track.

The Mechanics of Officiating: Field Events

Now it's time to move off the track and look at your work should you be assigned to the field event.

The Head Field Judge at Work Working under the supervision of the referee, you're the ranking official in the field events. It's your responsibility to (1) supervise the judges covering the various events, (2) see that the competition is fair to all contestants, and (3) see that the events start at their scheduled times or as soon thereafter as possible. On the latter point, however, please remember that no event may start ahead of its assigned time.

In addition to the above responsibilities, you hold several specific duties. You're to:

- Inspect and weigh all the field implements and apparatus prior to the events, seeing that they're up to regulation and in fit condition for use. Often, a *weights and measures official* is appointed for this task.
- Conduct a pregames meeting with all the event judges assigned to you, making certain that they all understand their duties and answering any questions that they may have concerning the supervision of their individual events. At this meeting, distribute the tapes necessary for measurements. They're to be obtained from—and returned to—the games committee.
- Verify all outstanding performances during the meet, especially those that may qualify as records.
- Check and certify the scorecards at the end of each event.
- Report to the referee for guidance or a decision on all matters, infractions, or irregularities on which you and the event judges cannot or are not permitted to decide.

The number of crews working under your supervision, of course, will depend on the number of events being contested. Each crew should be headed by one man—the chief event judge. He may be appointed by you or the games committee. Ideally, he should be the most experienced and knowledgeable man on the crew.

The Chief Event Judge As the official in charge of your event, you, of course, supervise the various judges under your command. You place them at their appropriate stations and, if the games committee hasn't already done so, assign them to their positions. You should report to your event site at least forty-five minutes before the first scheduled competition and be ready to:

- Inspect the site to make certain it's properly prepared and ready for the competition.
- Greet the competitors as they arrive, hold a roll call to make certain that everyone is present, and—unless the order of competition has been set by the games committee or the clerk of the course—supervise the drawing by lot that will establish the order. As is done on the track,

blank cartridges with numbers printed on their ends can be used in the drawing.
- See that the contestants start their warmups early enough to be completed prior to the start of the first competitions.

Though you're specifically charged with the above duties as chief of the crew, your fellow officials should lend you a hand in performing them and in helping in every other way possible to get the event started smoothly and on time. Once the meet starts, you're to see—again with the assistance of your crew—that it is conducted in accordance with the procedures established by the games committee. In keeping with those procedures, you're to:

- Be certain that the competition area is always free of noncompetitors.
- Call each contestant for his trial. In the vocabulary of track and field, a *trial* is the contestant's attempt in the event.
- Rule on whether some error by a contestant causes his trial to fail.
- Announce the distances or heights achieved. Each announcement should be made in a strong, clear voice.
- Keep a record of the heights and distances on your event card. At the end of the event, mark the card with the placement winners and submit it to the proper authority or the scorer.

When readying a contestant for his trial, you use two commands. The first is "Up," which summons him into place. The next is "On deck," which readies him for the trial and authorizes him to begin. At the end of the trial, things are officially wrapped up with the call, "In the hole."

In the next pages, we'll look at your crew's work on each event. But first, here are some general points on the conduct of the various events.

In the high jump and pole vault, the competitors are given three trials at each height. An individual is eliminated from the competition when he misses three consecutive trials at one height. The competition continues until all contestants are eliminated or until only one remains and can be designated the winner. In the event of a tie, the win goes to the contestant who suffered the fewest misses at the final height. If the tie can't be settled in this manner, then the athlete with the least number of unsuccessful vaults in the day's competition can be judged the winner. Still other methods for breaking ties are to be found in your rulebook.

In both events the beginning bar height is usually set by the games committee. If not, you're to choose a height that seems appropriate for the class of competition; be sure, though, not to set it so low that it doesn't challenge the best performers right from the start. In the high jump the bar may be raised in increments of one or two inches for subsequent trials. For the pole vault it may be raised six inches for the first and second trials; subsequent raises should be limited to three or four inches.

The long jump, triple jump, shot put, discus, and javelin events are all contested in one manner only. Each competitor is permitted three preliminary trials and three final trials. The winner is the athlete with the best efforts, whether they came in the preliminaries or the finals.

A word now on the order in which the youngsters compete: Depending on the type of meet being held and the number of contestants involved, various systems are used to establish the order of competition. In the high jump and pole vault events in dual meets, the competitors are often alternated. The visiting team is given the courtesy of choosing whether it wishes to be first or second in line. In very large meets the runners and vaulters frequently go off in flights of perhaps ten youngsters each; each flight performs until all the competitors have cleared the bar or have been eliminated.

In the other events—from the long jump to the javelin—the competitors commonly work in pairs. Each pair is given two trials in order before the next pair takes over. This procedure continues through the preliminary trials and then is continued in the finals. When pairing the youngsters, care should be taken to have the better performer (on the basis of his previous record) take his trial last so his partner doesn't tense up because of the challenge.

In all events, when setting the order of competition in the finals, again be sure to have the competitors with the best records perform last—and for the same reason.

Now for a look at each event:

At Work on the High Jump In this event the competitor must clear the crossbar on a jump launched from one foot. The trial fails when he:

- Displaces the crossbar as he attempts to clear it.
- Touches the ground beyond the crossbar or to its sides without clearing it.

• Approaches the bar and leaves the ground but fails to complete the jump.
• Clears the bar and lands in the pit only to stumble against the uprights to displace the bar or force himself to steady it.

You should measure the bar height at the start of the competition and decide on the increments for subsequent raises. When measuring, don't run the tape from the ground to the point where the bar intersects an upright. Take into account its natural sag and measure upwards to the bar's lowest point. To avoid delays, you needn't measure each new increment. A final measurement, of course, must be taken when the bar's maximum height has been determined.

Ideally, you should have two assistant judges and two helpers working with you. The crew positions are shown in the illustration. Yours is marked CJ.

Stationed at the upright opposite yours, assistant judge 1 watches the

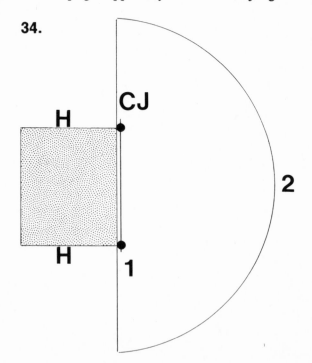

34.

crossbar to determine if it is displaced by actual contact. Assistant judge 2 controls the runway area and enforces the time limit granted each competitor for launching his run and jump. The helpers replace the fallen crossbar.

At Work on the Pole Vault Your position for this event, which calls for the competitor to clear the crossbar with the aid of a pole, is between one upright and the takeoff area. From there you watch the takeoff area to see that the vault is properly launched.

In essence the rules dictating a failed vault are the same as those for the high jump. The vaulter fails when he or the pole displaces the crossbar or when he enters the vault and then doesn't complete it. Additionally, a failed jump is called when:

- Any part of the vaulter's body—or the pole—touches the ground beyond the plane of the stopboard which is located in the takeoff area.

35.

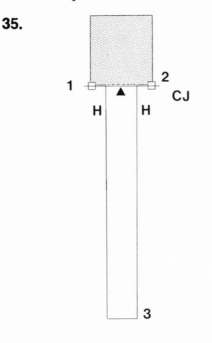

• The vaulter moves his top hand upward along the pole or shifts his lower hand to a spot above his upper hand during the jump.

As in the high jump, the crossbar height should be measured and the increments for raises established at the start of the event, and the bar measured again once the maximum height has been attained. Again, measure from the ground to the lowest point of the bar.

Working with you on the crew should be three assistant judges, plus two or three helpers to replace the fallen bar.

Assistant judges 1 and 2 determine contact with the bar and watch that the vaulter does not illegally shift his hands. Judge 3 manages the runway area and enforces the time limit. If there's a strong tailwind, judge 2 holds the additional job of catching the pole before it is pushed against the bar.

At Work on the Long Jump The long jump—or as it was once more widely called, the broad jump—is made from a takeoff board set at a prescribed distance from the landing pit. The edge of the board facing the pit is known as the *scratch line*. In boys' competition the scratch line is usually set twelve feet from the pit. Eight feet is the customary distance in girls' competitions.

Your position is directly alongside the takeoff board. When judging each trial, you must check that the competitor takes off from behind the scratch line or the scratch line extended (imaginary lines extending directly out to its sides). If the contestant's shoe goes across the line before he's airborne, the jump is declared a failure. It counts as a trial but is not measured.

It's also a failed jump if the competitor in landing loses control and leaves the pit closer to the front than to the rear. Again, it counts as a trial but goes unmeasured.

Each jump is measured on completion. The measurement is made by running the tape from the scratch line or the scratch line extended to the nearest point achieved by the jumper.

You should have three judges with you. A helper should be on hand to level the pit after each jump so the marks made by the next contestant can be clearly seen.

Assistant judges 1 and 2 are the officials who make each measurement. Judge 3 is in charge of the runway area and enforces the time limit. Judge 2 has the additional job of supervising the pit leveling.

36. **37.**

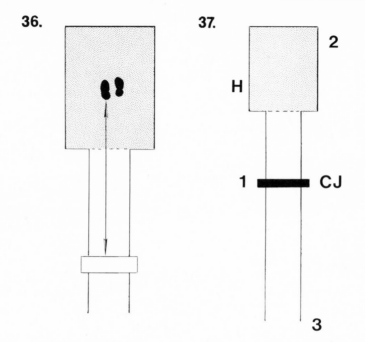

At Work on the Triple Jump With a couple of exceptions, the triple jump is the long jump's twin. It, too, is launched from a takeoff board set at a prescribed distance from the landing pit. The distance, however, is usually set at thirty to thirty-two feet for boys' competitions, and twenty-four feet for girls. Some officials feel that for safety's sake the distance for boys should never exceed thirty feet.

The rules governing a failed jump are the same as for the broad jump. The youngster must launch the jump from some point behind the stratch line or scratch line extended. He must land so that his exit is closer to the back of the pit than to the front.

But the jump itself bears little resemblance to the long jump. As its name indicates, it consists of three distinct moves, with one flowing directly from the other. On the first (called the *hop*), the youngster must land on the same foot used for the takeoff. On the second (the *step*), he must land on the opposite foot. In his final effort he lands on the foot of his choice.

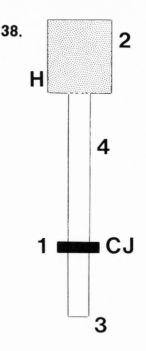

A miss on any of these actions results in a failed trial. As is usual on all failed long jumps, the trial counts but is not measured.

If working with an adequate crew, you'll have four assistant judges, plus one or two helpers to keep the pit leveled. Your duties and those of assistant judges 1, 2, and 3 are the same as on the long jump, as is the method of measurement. Judge 4 stands alongside the runway and checks that the three jumps are executed in their required sequence.

At Work on the Shot Put Working within a circle that measures seven feet in diameter, the contestant propels a metal ball (the *shot*) into a forty-five-degree sector extending outward from the center of the circle. In making his throw (the *put*), he must use a pushing action only.

Your position is outside and towards the back half of the circle. If the thrower fouls during or after the shot, you're to count the trial but not measure it. A foul is to be called when any of the following miscues shows up:

39.

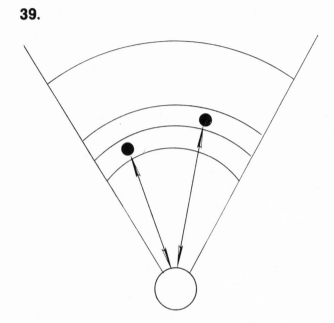

- The competitor, on taking his stance and placing the shot at or close to his chin, allows his hand to drop at any time during the throw.
- He throws—by some overarm action—rather than pushes the shot.
- He steps on or over the circle line during or after the throw. As seen in the illustration, a toe board may be placed against the forward half of the circle. His foot may touch the inside edge of the board. He may not touch the outside edge.
- The shot lands on or outside the sector—or foul—lines. The forty-five-degree sector is measured from the inner border of the lines.
- The competitor, on completing his throw, fails to leave the area via the back half of the circle.

The distance of the throw is measured from the rear edge of the point of contact. A tape measure is run from it to the inside edge of the circle nearest to the point of impact.

You'll need two assistant judges and two or three helpers. Assistant

40.

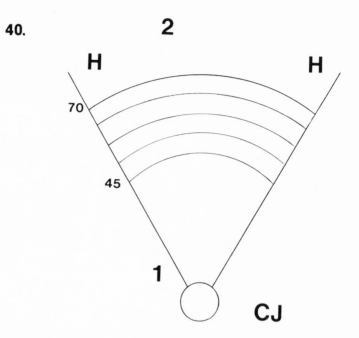

judge 1 enforces the time limit and joins judge 2 in making the measurement. Judge 2 is also responsible for determining the point of impact. The helpers fetch the shot and return it to the starting area. The return should be made along a route outside either foul line.

At Work on the Discus Except that a discus is thrown with a sidearm motion into a sixty-degree sector, this event exactly matches the shot put. The in-circle rules are the same, as are the rules calling for the discus to land inside the sector lines. Identical, too, is the procedure for measuring the distance achieved by each throw.

Finally, the same number of officials will be needed. Their individual duties will remain unchanged. But as the illustration shows, you will need to alter your position.

For the sake of making the record complete, the hammer throw should be mentioned here though it is not a routine feature in meets for younger

41.

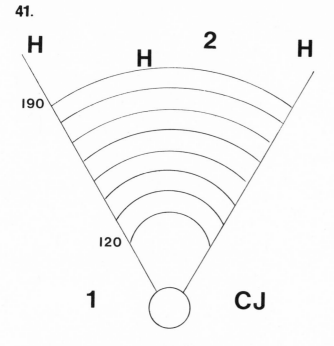

competitors. Should you run into it, however, it's to be officiated in the same manner as the shot put and the discus events.

At Work on the Javelin From behind an arced scratch line, the competitor in this event hurls a javelin into a triangular sector. The throw counts as a trial but is not measured if the javelin spears the ground on or outside the sector lines.

As in the long and triple jumps, your station is alongside the scratch line. As you watch the thrower, remember that the rules require him to hold the javelin by its whipcord grip. The thumb and forefinger, however, are allowed to touch the shaft. The same holds true for the forefinger and middle finger. An incorrect grip constitutes a foul, nullifies the measurement, and counts as a trial.

The thrower also draws a foul if he:

42.

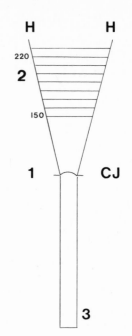

- Delivers the throw with anything but a motion that brings his arm up and above his shoulder.
- Executes a 360-degree turn before the javelin is airborne.
- Steps on or across the scratch line or the runway lines—or breaks their plane with any part of his body or apparel—before the throw is marked.

You should work with three assistant judges. Two workers are needed to return the javelins to the runway area.

Assistant judge 1 determines the impact point and then makes the measurement with judge 2. Judge 3 controls the runway area and enforces the time limit. The helpers are to return the javelins via a route outside the sector.

Your Uniform

There is no designated uniform for track and field officials, though large (and well-budgeted) meets often outfit the crews in jackets, shirts, or baseball-style caps all of the same color. In the absence of a uniform, all officials should dress neatly and, if possible, somewhat similarly so that they present a businesslike appearance that will contribute to the serious tenor of the games.

For purposes of easy identification, it's recommended that the starter wear a brightly colored jacket (red is suggested) or armband. The marshal and his crew should also be given identifying armbands or ribbons that can be attached to the sleeve.

A wide variety of equipment—ranging from the starting pistols to tape measures, record cards, and paper and pencils—is needed for a track meet of any size. It's to be provided by the games committee. Starters and judges will likely prefer to bring along their own whistles.

8. Volleyball

A VOLLEYBALL GAME can be handled by a varying number of officials ranging from a low of six to a high of ten. Most commonly, however, the officiating crew consists of eight people.

The Officials

On the eight-man crew are the *referee,* the *umpire,* four *line judges* (often, as in tennis, called linesmen), a *scorekeeper,* and a *timekeeper.* Two linesmen, rather than four, may be used. Let's begin with a general look at your duties at each spot.

The Referee Standing on a low platform (or perhaps a bench or chair) to one side of the net, you're the game's senior official. You're the official who supervises the progress of the game by ordering the ball served and by whistling it dead when a rally ends, a foul is committed, or a point is scored. You're also charged with watching for and penalizing a series of illegal player actions.

170

As senior official, you're also responsible for the supervision of your fellow crewmen. You have the authority to make final decisions on disagreements between them and on any questions not covered by the rules. You also have the authority—though you must exercise it carefully and diplomatically in the interests of cooperation—to overrule the decisions of any official.

Additionally, you hold a number of pregame responsibilities. You're called on to:

- Designate the line judges, the official scorekeeper, and the official timekeeper.
- Inspect the net and the court markings, at the same time checking on local ground rules and establishing any special rules that may seem necessary.
- Meet with your fellow officials to review their duties and inform them of any local ground rules and special rules that are to be observed.
- Meet with coaches and playing captains for a review of all pertinent rules.
- Inspect the balls available for use to see that they meet the necessary specifications. You then make the final decision on the game ball to be used.
- Supervise the coin toss between the team captains to decide service and choice of playing area.

If you're working under the rules for interscholastic competition, as published by The National Federation of State High School Associations, you and your fellow officials are to be in uniform and at the site of the match no later than twenty minutes before starting time. The coin toss is to take place at least fifteen minutes before game time.

The Umpire You work on the floor at the side of the net opposite the referee. Your chief responsibilities during play are to rule on player actions that may be out of the referee's view, to concentrate especially on the action between the spiking lines, and to control the entry of substitutes. Your job also calls for you to check and verify the score during time-outs and at the end of the game. When a team asks for a time-out, you're the official who informs its players of the number of time-outs legally remaining to them (each squad is permitted two in the course of a game). Like the referee, you hold several pregame duties. You're to:

- Meet with the scorekeeper and timekeeper for a review of their duties and a check of their equipment.
- Inspect the players' uniforms and equipment, making certain that they're up to regulation.
- Check the correctness of the teams' lineups.
- Assist the referee in his inspection of the net and the court markings.
- Assist him with the pregame conference with the coaches and playing captains.

Line Judges You and your three fellow linesmen work from positions just out of bounds. As shown in the illustration, you're stationed at the four corners of the court. At times when there aren't enough officials to go around (it happens), only two linesmen will be assigned to a game. Then you and your partner will work at the corners diagonally opposite each other.

As a line judge, you have just three game duties. First, when the ball lands in your area, you signal whether it is in or out of the court. Second, waving your arm overhead, you signal when a served or played ball is out of bounds when it crosses the net. Finally, you call last touches on balls going out of bounds.

When the serve is made from your area, you take on two additional tasks. You hold the ball during the time-out period preceding the serve. Then during the service itself, you check to see that the server remains in legal territory until the ball is away. Your pregame duties are just two. You're to attend the crew conference called by the referee and then review the limits of your responsibilities with your fellow linesmen. The limits are identical to those imposed on the tennis linesman: You're to be responsible for calls only in your own area but are to be ready to lend your companions a hand should they run into difficulty. But you're to assist them only if requested to do so. Unsolicited help is looked on as an intrusion.

The Scorekeeper You and the timekeeper watch the game from a table several feet off the umpire's side of the court. Your game responsibilities are several. You're charged with:

43.

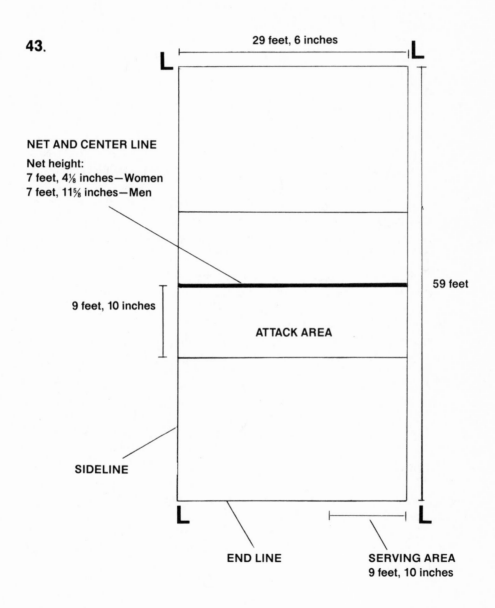

29 feet, 6 inches

L   L

NET AND CENTER LINE

Net height:
7 feet, 4⅛ inches—Women
7 feet, 11⅝ inches—Men

9 feet, 10 inches

ATTACK AREA

59 feet

SIDELINE

L   L

END LINE

SERVING AREA
9 feet, 10 inches

- Keeping a record of individual and team scoring.
- Verifying the serving order to the referee.
- Reporting the proper serving order to the referee or the umpire during dead-ball periods.
- Keeping a record of the time-outs charged to each team (two per game, remember) and notifying the umpire when a third is requested.
- Maintaining a record of the substitutions made by each team. You must immediately notify the umpire when a substitution is for (1) a wrong entry, (2) a wrong position, (3) the re-entry of a disqualified player, and (4) the re-entry of an injured player who was replaced by a player who had already entered another position. Each player is allowed three entries in a game; you must not count an illegal substitution as one of those entries.
- Notifying the umpire during the first dead-ball period when there is disagreement or confusion concerning the score.
- Operating the automatic scoring device. If a manual scoring device is being used instead, you direct an assistant when to make changes in it.

Like the line umpire, you have two pregame tasks. You're to review your duties with the umpire and then check to be certain that your equipment is in proper working order.

The Timekeeper You're seated with the scorekeeper at the off-court table. Your basic job is to operate the game's timing device. With it, you're to:

- Time the length of each time-out. The length of a time-out depends on your league policy; United States Volleyball Association rules limit it to thirty seconds while the rules published by the National Federation of State High School Associations say that it may not run beyond sixty seconds. You must inform the court when fifteen seconds remain to the resumption of play.
- Time the intermission between games. It is usually limited to three minutes. Again, you must signal the court when fifteen seconds remain to the resumption of play.
- Signal the ends of the time-out and intermission periods with an audio device. If possible, the audio device should not be a whistle so that it won't be confused with those belonging to the referee and umpire. Customarily, a horn or buzzer is used.

These three duties all refer to timing when the ball is not actually in play. So far as actual play is concerned, a volleyball game may be either timed or untimed. When untimed, the game is played, no matter how long it takes, until one team tallies fifteen points and holds a two-point advantage over its opponent. A timed game, which is usually a feature of tournaments that must work their way through a heavy schedule of matches, goes to the team that has a two-point advantage at the first dead ball period after eight minutes of play; if no one has the advantage at that time, the game continues until the advantage is won.

In timed games you become one of the most important officials on the court. You're charged with starting the timing device in the instant of each service—and with killing the time in the instant a whistle ends the action. Additionally, you continue to time the intermission and time-out periods. Finally, you sound the end of the game with your audio device.

For total accuracy, you'll need to use not only the timing device but a stopwatch. Use the timing device for the moments of actual playing time. Save the stopwatch for the intermissions and time-outs.

The Mechanics of Officiating

To see the procedures and techniques used in volleyball officiating, let's put you first in the referee's spot.

The Referee at Work Positioned at the side of the net, you spend the game on a low platform of some sort, perhaps a bench, perhaps even a chair. Your head should be about two to three feet above the net, giving you an overall view of the court.

The game begins—and play resumes after every dead-ball period—with a service by one of the teams. The service is made on your command only. To initiate a service, first ask each captain if his team is ready to play; an affirmative reply will be an upraised arm. Immediately point to the server and then execute the *serve* signal (an easy sweep of the arm towards the opposing side). Simultaneously, there should be a short blast on your whistle.

Prior to and at the moment of service, check to see that the players on the serving team are properly positioned (don't worry about the receiving players; the umpire is attending to them). The players can be incorrectly positioned in a number of ways. For instance, the server may be serving out of turn. There may be a player on the court who is an illegal substitution. Or there may be such illegal alignments as screening or overlapping.

Should you glimpse something amiss, immediately give two short blasts on the whistle. Extend both arms out to the sides as a signal to halt the service. The penalty is then to be a *side-out* (the loss of service for the team). If the umpire sights incorrectly positioned players on the receiving side, the penalty is usually a point awarded to the serving team.

Once the ball is properly served, keep your eye on it and watch for:

- Foot faults. Basically, you have to deal with just two infractions here. It's a foot fault when the server steps out of the service area. And it's a foot fault when a player, while making or attempting to make a play, steps on or over a court line which defines an area in which his movement is restricted or prohibited. The lines involved are the spiking lines and the center line.
- Net fouls. You'll see these when a player interferes with an opponent, touches the net or net supports, runs into your platform, or illegally reaches over the net. Remember, though, that there are two instances in which the player may legally reach over the net. He can do so on blocks or attempted blocks and when following through after hitting or trying to hit the ball.
- Double fouls: It's a double foul when two opposing players commit an infraction in the same instant.
- Illegal ball handling: This will likely be your most difficult call. The technicalities involved are several and so it will have a section to itself later in the chapter.

Now for some pointers: First, the ball must safely clear the net on the serve; if it touches the net in even the slightest degree, the action is to be whistled dead. But it can be a problem to sight those light touches—those "ticks," as they're called. To make certain they're detected, place one hand lightly on the net cable just before the serve. You'll have no trouble picking up any tick whatsoever. Once the serve has cleared the net, withdraw your hand. The ball is now free to touch the net in passing with play continuing until the rally ends.

Next, it's possible to become confused over which team is serving. Any of several techniques may be used to keep things straight. Some referees hold the whistle in the side of the mouth towards the serving team. Others place a foot forward on the server's side. Still others lightly fist the hand on the server's side. One of the most popular techniques is to drape a towel over the net with the long side facing the server.

Net fouls, especially those that send a player's hand over the net, can be hard to see. They're best sighted by crouching down and sighting right along the net cable. As soon as you detect a foul, sound the whistle and stop the action. Give the *net foul* signal (a hand placed alongside the net on the offending team's side), point to the player responsible, and announce him by number—for instance, "Number three over."

It's also no easy trick to follow the ball. Here, you'll need to use what is called peripheral vision. This means that you must track the ball itself and simultaneously extend your vision so you can accurately judge the spot where it will fall. Only by sighting in on that spot at the time the ball arrives—or, better yet, in the instant before—will you be set to pick up fouling actions.

As is true in all sports, you must call only the infractions that you actually see. If you're screened from a given action, don't guess but leave the call to a better positioned colleague. And, of course, never anticipate a foul; some last-second movement may make everything legal. Wait until the foul occurs. Then call it.

There will be times, however, when you or a fellow official mistakenly whistle the ball dead. This occurs most often because of anticipated calls. On a mistaken whistle, you have but one choice. Summon the team captains, honestly admit the muff, and call for a replay. Signal for a replay by clasping both hands together in front of the net post.

You may also call for a replay in a number of other circumstances. A replay is appropriate in certain double-foul cases, and the only possible way out of things when a foreign object enters the court, when there is a nonfoul player injury, or when your fellow officials come up with conflicting calls that you can't resolve.

There's yet another common error that you must handle. On the serve, an official sometimes misses such infractions as an illegally substituted player or a server who is working out of turn. These problems are to be taken care of—and the proper penalty imposed—as soon as there's a dead-ball period.

The Umpire at Work   Your responsibilities dovetail with those of the referee. Prior to any serve, you watch for violations of player positioning by the receiving team while he keeps an eye on the serving unit. Once the ball is served, your attention shifts mainly to the area between the spiking lines, and you join him in checking for foot faults at the center and spiking lines, for net fouls, and for ballhandling miscues.

You're free to move back and forth along the court to arrive at the most advantageous positions for viewing the action, but your movements should be restricted to the area between the spiking lines. When the play comes to the net, station yourself there and watch for "lower down" fouls—namely, foot faults across the centerline, interference below the net, and fouls away from the action on the ball. Unless otherwise instructed, leave the problem of hands-over-the-net to the referee. From his raised position, he's in the best spot to see them.

"Assistance to the referee" should be a key phrase in your officiating vocabulary. Help him in every way possible. Repeat his signals for point, side-out, and substitutions so that there's no chance they'll be missed by anyone (it's not necessary, however, to repeat his signals for fouls or for a service). Always remember that despite his elevated station, he's locked into a stationary position and can be easily screened from some vital action. So never let your guard down. Keep your eyes open at all times and be ready to pick up on any call that he may miss.

The Line Judge at Work   You're stationed at one of the four corners of the court and charged with the primary responsibility of judging whether a ball landing in your area is in or out of bounds. Your area covers the end line and the sideline directly to your front. For the best view of the action, you should stand about three feet from the corner of the court and safely back from the line. You're then free to move about in search of the best vantage point from which to see the action. Whether standing still or moving, take care to avoid interfering with the players or being struck by the ball. Never enter the court during live-ball action.

Whenever the ball lands in your area, you must signal whether it is in or out of the court. To be out of bounds, the ball must touch beyond the sideline or the end line; it's inbounds if it hits the line itself. You're to point down and towards the court for *in* balls. An upraised arm is the *out* signal. (Depending on your association, you may be given a signal flag;

the signals remain the same.) The main point to remember is that a signal must always be made even if the ball is well above your head as it travels out of bounds.

Depending again on your association, you may need to keep track of the last player to touch the ball in your area before it goes out of bounds. In some organizations, you're expected to take on this task. But the United States Volleyball Association calls for you to do so only at the request of the referee.

When the ball is served from your area, yours is the job of watching for a server foot fault. He must not step on or over the end line prior to the serve. If he does, move immediately onto the court, raise both arms to catch the referee's attention, and then signal the infraction by pointing to your foot.

Your surveillance of the sideline includes watching the ball as it crosses the net near the sideline marker. If the ball is over or inside the marker, it's inbounds. But if it flies to the outside, you've got an out-of-bounds call on your hands. Up goes the arm.

At the end of each game, you and the linesman across the court are to change sides. The same goes at the midway point in the final game. The changes are made so that you'll have the same relative position to the team throughout the match.

The rules of courtesy advised for tennis linesmen also apply to you. Avoid talking to your fellow linesmen during the match. And above all, make no comments on the game or on individual performances. In a word, do or say nothing that will distract or upset the players.

Whistles and Signals

The official's whistle is bound to be heard repeatedly in the course of a game. Sounded as often as it is, the whistle can be a nerve-wracking thing if its blasts are continually prolonged and shrilly full-powered. Good officiating technique calls for the blasts to be short and varied in strength. For instance, a soft whistle is fine when signaling a serve; just enough sound is needed to get the server's attention. A soft blast will also do nicely for served balls that clearly hit the net and for balls that are a mile out of bounds. Save the sharp blasts for fouls, especially those that occur when play is at its hottest.

44.

VOLLEYBALL SIGNALS

Illegal Alignment · Foot Fault · Illegal Hit or Serve

In-Bounds · Out-of-Bounds · Begin Service

Net Foul · Side-out · Point · Time-Out

Unsportsmanlike Conduct · Ball Touched · Replay · Unnecessary Delay

Substitution · Illegal Substitution · Four Hits · Double Hit

From *Volleyball Rulebook*, The National Federation of State High School Assn's

Depending on your association, there can be well over fifteen hand signals in volleyball. Be sure to execute them clearly and decisively. You'll find that the signals will be most widely seen by players and spectators alike if you hold back on them until just the right moment. It's that moment following a score or a whistle when the players and the spectators instinctively turn to you.

Handling Fouls and Penalties

There are two basic penalties in volleyball. If the serving team fouls (the United States Volleyball Association uses the much gentler term, *faults*), it is assessed a side-out, with the service then going to the receiving team. Should the receivers foul, a point is awarded to the serving team. In addition, some associations penalize a team for a multiple foul—more than one infraction committed by teammates during a deadball period—by taking away one of its charged time-outs.

Under certain circumstances a team can also be penalized with a loss of points. To repeat a statement made earlier, play is to be stopped immediately when a player is found to be serving out of turn; the same goes when a player has re-entered the game at a position not his own or has re-entered too many times. But suppose that the player is on the receiving team and the error goes unnoticed until his squad tallies one or more points. If the discovery is made while his team is still serving, those points must be canceled and the service handed to the opposition.

If the discovery comes after the service has changed hands in the normal course of play, however, nothing is to be done. You're to let the score stand but correct the error.

Unsportsmanlike conduct by players and coaches earns a penalty and, in time, can see the guilty party disqualified. Acts of unsportsmanlike conduct by players include play that incites roughness, the use of words or gestures intended to disconcert an opponent playing the ball, and derogatory remarks aimed at the officials. For the coach, unsportsmanlike conduct ranges from entering the court during play to addressing an official disrespectfully or attempting to influence his decisions.

Customarily, the first incident of unsportsmanlike conduct brings a warning from the referee. The second earns a penalty. Persistent misconduct can result in disqualification.

As referee, you can also react to an unruly crowd by suspending play. For the safety of the game and the players, you're authorized to postpone play until the proper degree of order is reinstated. The host school or club is responsible for restoring the order and keeping the spectators under control.

Playing faults and unsportsmanlike conduct are not the only occurrences that bring a penalty. You're also to penalize for violations of the charged time-out rule. Each team is permitted two time-outs per game, with the length of each determined by league policy. If a team delays in restarting play at the end of a time-out, you're to charge it with another time-out, which it then may take. If the team has already used its allotted time-outs, then you're to penalize with a side-out or a point.

Finally, you have the authority as referee to forfeit a game when a team fails to appear at the match on time, fails to have sufficient players at game time, or fails to continue play when you so direct.

Only three points can be made concerning your method of administering penalties. First, of course, never call a fault unless you actually see it; no anticipation, please, and no effort to even things up with your calls. Second, be decisive in your judgments and clear in your signals. And, finally, though decisive, always be courteous and objective when making a call. Even when penalizing for continued misconduct, avoid showing any hint of anger towards the player involved. Anger can upset his teammates by making them think you've turned against them, and your next close calls may trigger protests.

Problem Calls

Two fouls will likely give you more trouble than all the others put together. Both are ballhandling infractions. One has to do with the way the player touches the ball. The other concerns the number of times that he and his team may touch it in succession.

Player Touches The rules state that the ball may be touched only by a body part or parts at or above the waist. They also stress that the contact must be brief and instantaneous, with the ball bounding away cleanly. The player must not allow the ball to come to rest in his hands even momentarily. He must hit it and neither push nor carry it forward.

With the game proceeding at its traditional swift pace, the job of calling a push or a carry can be difficult. Five suggestions, however, should prove of great help here:

- On underhand hits, pay special attention to the player's wrists and fingers. It's almost certainly a foul when they flex and follow the ball as it rises.
- On overhand hits, the fingers and palms should be watched. If they follow the ball, seeming to push it along, call the foul.
- On spikes, again watch the palms and wrists for a following action. A push is most likely to occur when the player drives the ball downward with both hands.
- Always remember that, despite the rules, there are times when it's physically impossible for the player to return the ball without having it remain an instant in his hands. This often happens as he's playing the ball from below or jumping high, when the ball is set, or after it's been hit hard to him. He's *not* to be penalized here.
- Nor, if he makes the hit correctly, should he be penalized for moving his hands backwards—and perhaps giving a mistaken impression of holding—during or after a hit.

Number of Touches   The rules stipulate that no player may touch or be touched by the ball twice in succession. A teammate or an opponent must play the ball in the interim before he goes near it again. There are, however, exceptions to the rule. They make its enforcement a headache because they can be difficult to see and judge. You must be constantly on the lookout for them.

Let's look first at the exceptions that enable the player *to touch* the ball twice in a row:

- A second contact is legal after two opponents simultaneously touch the ball. Either man may play the ball immediately so long as it falls on his side of the court. The touch counts as his *first*.
- Likewise, a second contact is legal if two teammates simultaneously touch the ball. Either player may hit it. The touch here counts as the man's *second*.

- A player may play the ball a second time if he's involved in a block. Again, the touch is his *second.*

And now the exceptions that permit a man to *be touched* twice in succession:

- The ball is permitted to rebound from one body part to another on one attempt to play a spiked ball that has not already been touched by another player. This multiple touch counts as the player's first, after which the ball must be touched by another player. There's an exception within the exception: the ball in this instance may not bounce from one hand or forearm to another hand or forearm.
- The ball may touch more than one body part during a player's one attempt to block.

While the player may not touch or be touched twice in succession, the team is permitted to touch the ball no more than three times before sending it back across the net. There are, of course, exceptions—two in all. The team may have more than three touches if (1) there is a simultaneous contact by opponents or (2) the first touch is an action to block. In each case, the touch doesn't count. The next touch is counted.

Both the referee and the umpire should keep track of touches, but, as referee, you're primarily responsible for counting team touches. When you see more than the permitted three, sound your whistle and raise your right hand, extending four fingers to indicate the fourth touch.

Your Uniform

Your exact uniform will be determined by the regulations of your league. If you're working, say, under the rules published by the National Federation of State High School Associations, you'll be expected to wear a black-and-white vertically striped shirt; black slacks, culottes, or skirt; and gym shoes and socks. Under the same rules, you may also wear navy blue and white uniforms. Shoes and socks may be either white or black, but should match each other.

But if you're working under United States Volleyball Association rules, your shirt will be all white and short-sleeved, with the USVBA emblem on the right sleeve and the association's referee emblem over the left chest. Black slacks and a black belt are worn by both men and women, as are low-cut white tennis shoes and white athletic socks.

No matter the association, all officials should carry a whistle on a cord. It helps avoid confusion if the sounds of the line judges' whistles are slightly different from those of the referee and umpire.

9. Swimming and Diving

SWIMMING AND DIVING meets are held under the auspices of a number of associations, among them the National Collegiate Athletic Association (NCAA), the Amateur Athletic Union (AAU), and the National Federation of State High School Associations (NFSHSA). The officiating procedures and techniques vary somewhat among the associations, with each organization having its own approaches to the supervision of a meet. This chapter, then, must limit itself to general material that will give you a basic beginning idea of the officials needed and their work. The individual requirements of your particular association are to be found in your rulebook.

The Officials

As in track and field, the number of officials required at poolside hinges much on the size of the meet. Basically, at least twelve positions should be filled, with the size of the crew then swelling as assistants are added. The basic positions are:

1. The *referee*
2. The *starter*
3. *Lane judges*
4. The *chief timer* and assistants
5. *Stroke inspectors*
6. *Turn judges*
7. *Takeoff judges* for relay events
8. The *diving referee*
9. *Diving judges*
10. The *scorer*
11. The *meet announcer*
12. *Automatic timer operators* if such timers are used.

To this list can be added a number of positions that while not mandatory can certainly help things run more efficiently and smoothly. For instance, the scorer may be assigned an assistant who helps him make his computations. Runners may be used to carry decisions from the judges to the scoring table. It's nice to have a press steward to keep reporters posted on the progress of the meet. There can also be a custodian of awards to supervise the presentation of trophies and medals. And it's good to have a doctor to attend to medical emergencies.

Swimming and diving meets are customarily planned and presented by a meet committee, headed by a meet director. When planning a championship competition, the director will have to fill the twelve listed positions with individual crewmen. But in organizing a dual meet, he can combine some of the jobs and assign them to one man. It's common practice, for example, to have the meet referee serve as the starter in dual meets. He may also be asked to become a stroke inspector or the diving referee.

The Meet Referee Your duties are similar to those of your counterpart in track and field. Unless otherwise requested, you're not expected to judge any of the competitions but are in overall charge of the day's proceedings, supervising the officiating crew, enforcing the rules, and seeing that all runs smoothly and without delay. In nonchampionship gatherings, you decide all questions not covered by the rules; in championship meets, this job is usually left to the director or a special committee.

Your overall supervisory responsibilities break down into specific pre-meet and meet duties. The former call for you to:

- Make certain the pool is properly marked and ready for use.
- Inspect all meet equipment, seeing that it is up to standard and in its proper place.
- Assign your fellow officials to their specific jobs if the director has not already done so and review with them their duties and responsibilities. Because of the number of officials needed, you may face the same problem as the track and field referee: the necessity of working with some inexperienced personnel. If so, you'll need to spend some time coaching them how best to do their jobs.

Ordinarily, you're expected to arrive at least thirty minutes before the first event so you'll have sufficient time to handle your various tasks. If you know that you have inexperienced people on your hands, try to arrive even earlier. (The best idea here—and in track and field—is to hold a clinic or an instructional class some days ahead of time for the inexperienced personnel.)

If you're involved in a championship meet, the rules call for you to hold a premeet conference with the team captains and the starter. The purpose is to go over meet procedures with them and alert them to any special circumstances that may prevail. Everyone's questions should be answered fully.

Now for your work during the meet itself. Your overall supervision includes such specifics as (1) making certain that all the events are held on schedule, (2) seeing that the results of each event are quickly reported to the scorer and the meet announcer, (3) ordering the events to begin promptly if any competitors are late in arriving, and (4) curtailing the use of horns, bells, sirens, and other noisemakers by the spectators.

In addition to these duties, you directly supervise the swimming events. Direct supervision of the diving competition is left to the diving referee (remember, in dual meets, you may end up with both jobs). As part of your swimming duties, you're to:

- Check the youngsters as they take their places at their proper lanes and have them position themselves on the pool deck or starting platform.

Once the swimmers are in place, turn them over to the starter. Some meets have a *clerk of the course*. When he is present, he takes over this job.

- Watch the start to see that it's properly made if there is not a *recall* (assistant) *starter* at hand for this purpose. Should you glimpse a false start that's missed by the starter, signal him immediately. When the field is recalled for a fresh try, you or the starter should notify the swimmer responsible for the trouble and warn him that two false starts will see him disqualified from the race.
- Signal any infraction that you see during the race. The signal is a hand raised overhead with the palm open.
- Notify the competitors involved and/or their coaches of any infractions observed and inform them of the resulting disqualifications. The notification is to be made immediately after the race. In practice, this job can be handled by you or the starter, or by the two of you together.
- Settle any disagreement over one event prior to the start of the next.

Your day ends when you check the swimming scores as tabulated by the scorer and, on finding everything in order, sign the scoresheet. With your signature the score becomes official and cannot be changed if later found to be in error.

The officials working under your jurisdiction can be subdivided as they are in track and field. Some work just the swimming events while others handle the diving competition. (Of course, in smaller meets many of the officials can do double duty, covering both swimming and diving, as long as there is no time conflict.) Several officials provide what can be called general services.

The Officials: Swimming Events

The officials who handle the swimming events are (1) the starter, (2) the lane judges, (3) the chief timer and assistants, (4) the stroke inspectors, (5) the turn judges, and (6) the takeoff judges.

The events may also be served by a *clerk of the course* especially in a championship meet. If so, he's looked on as the referee's good right arm. He helps check the swimmers into their assigned lanes prior to each race and provides the meet announcer with the details necessary for introducing each event. The clerk may also do the same work for the diving competition.

The Starter As starter, you take control of the swimmers once the referee has directed them to the starting line and surrendered them to you. Your job is to launch each race in a manner that is fair to all competitors, recalling them for a fresh try if there is a false (premature) start. On long races (the 500-yard freestyle, for example), you fire a pistol to indicate when the lead swimmer has two laps remaining. The shot must be timed so it's heard as the leader is five yards from turning into the final laps.

Finish Judges You and your fellow judges watch the finish line to determine the order of placements. Often, a meet will have a *head lane judge* to supervise the crew. The number of judges working with you depends on the type of meet being held and its size. In dual meets two judges may be assigned to pick first place, with one each assigned to subsequent placements. In championships two judges are assigned to each lane.

The Chief Timer Along with the judges, you and your assistants watch the finish line, your job being to record the times posted by the swimmers. Your crew can be the most sizable in the meet. Three timers should be assigned to each lane, meaning you'll need twenty-four helpers if all eight lanes are in use.

Stroke Inspectors You're to watch the swimmers and be alert for violations in strokes, kicks, and body positions. The number of inspectors used depends on the rules of your association. Some associations want an inspector per lane in championship meets. For instance, the rules published by the National Federation of State High School Associations (NFSHSA) call for two inspectors at a championship meet. Moving along the length of the pool, they divide the lanes between themselves with each man responsible for the swimmers closest to him.

Turn Judges Just as your title indicates, you watch the turns and pushoffs to see that they're properly executed. Ideally, there should be one judge per lane. In championships it's common practice not only to assign a judge to each lane but to have him also work as a stroke inspector. In smaller meets, you may need to work alone or with a partner, moving from lane to lane as the swimmers arrive. In smaller meets the starter often doubles as a stroke inspector and/or turn judge.

Takeoff Judges You work the relay races only. You're to see that each swimmer on the team does not leave the starting mark until the preceding swimmer touches the end of the pool. In championships there should definitely be one judge per lane being used. Two judges, standing to either side of the pool and dividing the lanes between themselves, can get the job done in dual meets.

The Officials: Diving Events

The diving events are officiated by the diving referee and the diving judges.

The Referee of Diving Yours is the job of supervising the diving competitions, advising the judges of mandatory point losses on certain infractions, and seeing that everything is conducted in accordance with your association rules. You may also serve as one of the judges during a dual meet. You should never do so, however, at a championship meet.

The Diving Judges With your fellow judges, you evaluate each dive and award it a point score. The score ranges from a high of ten down to zero. Your crew should not number below five people at championships. A minimum of three is needed at a dual meet.

The Officials: General Services

The scorer and the meet announcer are the officials who provide general services.

The Scorer As scorer, you're given four basic jobs. You (1) record the official times in the swimming events and the order of finish in both the swimming and diving events, (2) assist in the tabulation of the diving scores, (3) maintain a record of the cumulative team scores, and (4) operate the scoreboard or, as it's called in the rules, the visible scoring device.

If possible, you should have at least two assistants with one assigned to operate the scoreboard so you're left free for the more demanding job of computing the event results and team standings; you will, however, be responsible for supervising his work. The second assistant is a must at championships. Called the *recorder,* he helps you (or takes on the whole job) of calculating the points that establish individual and team standings and that, at times, must be used to determine the order of finish in the swimming events.

The point system used in swimming events can tax the memory. To begin, in dual meets, the actual number of points awarded usually hinges on the number of lanes being used. The rulebook published by the NFSHSA, for example, calls for dual meets to be scored as follows:

Individual Events

	1st	2nd	3rd	4th	5th	6th	7th	8th
8 lanes	8	6	5	4	3	2	1	0
6 lanes	6	4	3	2	1	0		
4 lanes	4	2	1	0				

Relays

	1st	2nd	3rd	4th
8 lanes	10	5	3	0
6 lanes	8	4	2	0
4 lanes	6	3	1	

Further, the number of points awarded changes when you come up against a championship meet or a nonchampionship affair involving three or more teams. Finally, things can become downright complicated when the swimmers are so tightly bunched at the end of a race that the order of finish can't be firmly determined by the lane judges. A separate scoring procedure, called the ballot system, then comes into play. We'll talk more of it later in the section on the mechanics of officiating.

You must be thoroughly acquainted with your association's methods of scoring and should have the rulebook within easy reach at all times for quick reference. It goes without saying that your job requires someone who's intelligent, good with figures, and able to work swiftly and accurately. In dual meets, the referee often fills in as the scorer.

The Meet Announcer You're a carbon copy of the track and field announcer. Stationed at a public address microphone, you announce each upcoming event, naming the competitors and, if it's a race, their lanes. Throughout the day you keep the spectators abreast of the event results and the latest team standings. Between times, you provide them with information about conveniences (the location of restrooms, exits, refreshment stands, and such). Finally, at the close of the meet you announce the final scores and introduce any competitors who are to receive awards.

The Mechanics of Officiating: Swimming Events

Now we come to the procedures and techniques that have been developed over the years to help the officials do their jobs smoothly and efficiently. Let's take a look at each officiating station.

The Starter at Work Your working location is at poolside, a short distance to the front of the starting marks. It's recommended that you stand about ten feet out from the marks, but you're free to choose a spot as close in as three feet or as far away as twenty. Whatever spot you select, it should be one that gives you a comfortable view of all the swimmers.

Like your counterpart in track and field, you launch each race with a pistol shot. The gun used should be the type that can be cocked for instant firing. A .38 caliber gun is advised for outdoor meets, and a .22 caliber for indoor pools. The starting gun may be used for recalls on false starts. If you wish, you may turn to a second gun or a whistle for the recalls.

The swimmers are in the hands of the referee when they gather at the starting blocks. He checks lane assignments and sets the youngsters in place, at last signaling you to take over. He may handle the instructions for the race or leave them to you; he should tell you of his choice before the day begins. If the instructions are left to you, you're to announce (1) the distance to be covered and the point where the race will end, (2) the stroke requirements, and (3) the signal that will be used to start the race.

Be sure to speak loudly and clearly—especially when contending with the roar characteristic of indoor pools—so that you can be heard and understood in the most distant lanes. But speak in a calm and friendly fashion. Always understand that you've got a group of keyed-up youngsters in your care; do nothing that will add to their nervousness and perhaps cause a false or late start. It's traditional to attract their attention at first by calling, "Quiet on the start."

Two types of start—standing and backstroke—are used in swimming events. Both are launched with the single command, "Take your mark," followed in an instant by a gunshot. Let's look at each in turn.

For the standing start, each swimmer must first stand erect with his feet on the starting line. When you call "Take your mark," all must immediately enter the starting position and remain in it, motionless, until the gunshot. Before firing, quickly check that no one is moving in the least. In particular, be on the alert for the youngster who, though seeming to be motionless, is actually continuing to inch downward in a "rolling start." He's hoping to be starting a recoil just as the gun sounds. If successful, he'll have an instant's advantage over the rest of the field.

When competing in the backstroke event, the swimmers line up in the water. They face the starting marks, with both hands grasping the pool edge (or the starting grips) and both feet in contact with the pool wall. On the "take your mark" command, each swimmer enters a starting position comfortable to him. It must be one that does not lift him completely out of the water or cause him to remove both hands or both feet from the pool end.

On all starts, the swimmers must respond immediately to your voice command; a delay in entering the starting position constitutes a false start. If you see a delay or a failure to hold the starting position properly, call things off with the command, "Stand up." Have the swimmers relax a moment and then, after the youngster responsible for the trouble has been warned, start again. Once the "take your mark" command is given, you should wait no more than a second or two before firing the gun.

When there is a false start at takeoff, immediately fire the recall gun or sound your whistle. At the same time, signal for the recall rope to be dropped. It extends across midpool and is needed for those swimmers who fail to hear the recall.

The Head Lane Judge at Work As was said earlier, some meets have a head lane judge to supervise the lane crews. Actually, due to the growing use of automatic timing devices to determine the order of finish, the head lane judge seems not as much needed as in the past. But his work must be mentioned here because he still plays a major role in small meets and in communities where timing devices have yet to be installed.

Should the job of head lane judge fall to you, you'll find that the actual mechanics of your work will depend on whether your crew is working a dual or championship meet.

In a dual meet, you might have two judges on hand to pick first place, and one for each subsequent placement. On first meeting your crew, you're to assign them to their individual placements (if the meet director or referee hasn't already done so), provide them with the cards on which they'll write their decisions, and position them at poolside. They're to be stationed to either side of the finish line and should be divided into two equal groups. Double-check to see that the first-place judges always work at opposite sides of the pool. If you're lucky, there will be staircase-type risers available; the judges can then stand on the steps, one above the other, for a good overall view of the finish line.

In common with the finish judges in track and field, they may watch the approach of the swimmers. In the last moments, each crewman should make an effort to narrow down the field of swimmers actively contesting the placement he's judging. Then his eyes go to the finish line and remain there until he sees his placement touch the finish pad. He immediately writes the swimmer's lane number on his card, doing so without consulting any of his fellow judges or attempting to see what they are writing. His choice must be his alone and must not be influenced from the outside.

When all the cards are filled out, they come to you for the tabulation establishing the order of finish. At times, especially on bunched finishes, you're apt to run into disagreements among the judges. For example, the second- and third-place judges may select the same swimmer. To settle matters, you must follow what is known as numerical order, meaning that the higher-placed judge's decision takes precedence. In this instance, the second-place spot would go to the swimmer.

Regardless of whether your crewmen are newcomers or veterans, you should spend a few moments coaching them in their duties before taking them out to poolside. In particular, urge them not to forget the outside lanes on close finishes; the fastest swimmers are usually assigned the center lanes, and so it can be easy to overlook the competitors on the fringe. And remind them to be always on the alert for those hard-to-see underwater touches at the finish line.

Now let's talk about a championship meet. Here, you have two judges per lane. Each two-man team is split and placed on opposite sides of the pool, their sole job being to determine the placement in their lane. Each man is to record the highest placement that he sees in the lane; this means that if he thinks his swimmer ends in a tie for first place with a competitor, he's to mark him for first place; the same goes for a tie in any other placement. Again, he's to write down his choice without referring to his fellow judges. Again, when the cards are filled out, they come to you for tabulation.

Should you run into disagreements—and they'll likely be the rule rather than the exception in tight finishes—they're to be settled by what is called the ballot system. The system calls for the cards to go immediately to the scorer's table. There they are reviewed, and each swimmer is awarded a certain number of points for each placement he was given— one point for first, two for second, three for third, and so on. Simultaneously, the official times recorded for the swimmers are checked and similarly pointed. When all the points are computed, the swimmer with the lowest score emerges as the winner. The subsequent placements follow along an ascending scale.

In recent years, fully automatic and semi-automatic timing devices have been coming into increasing use. Showing the swimming times to a fraction of a second and accurately establishing the order of finish, they're a boon to competition. But they may seem about to put your judges and the timing crews out of business. Well, don't worry. Lane judges and timers are still needed.

A fully automatic device triggers itself on the starter's gun and stops as each swimmer, in turn, touches the finish pad. But the judges and timers still must keep an eye on things. Their readings will be needed if the equipment fails.

A semi-automatic device may be used by itself or as a backup system for a fully automatic unit. It may start automatically with the gun or be triggered manually. But it does not stop automatically. One judge in each lane stops it by pressing a button in the instant that the finish pad in his lane is touched. Again, judging and timing readings must be used if there's an equipment failure.

The Chief Timer at Work Your work begins when you divide the officials under you into crews of three men each. Each crew is assigned a lane and is positioned directly above it at the finish line. Each man on the crew carries a stopwatch, with the official time for the lane being determined by a comparison of the watch readings. A fourth timer may be assigned to record split times.

One man on each crew should be put in charge and designated the *head lane timer*. Once the races start, each threesome should work just as their counterparts in track and field do. They should hold their watches so that the stems can be triggered not with the thumb but with the faster-reacting forefinger. On the starter's command, "Take your mark," the stems are to be depressed until all slack is gone and then triggered instantly with the sound of the gun. As their swimmer approaches the finish line, the three timers again depress the stems to the limit of the slack so there will be no delay in stopping the watches when the pad is touched.

As soon as the watches are stopped, the head lane timer marks the three readings on a card, compares them, establishes the official time for the lane, and delivers the card to you. Should he find the readings to be exactly the same, there will be no question about the time. But it's more likely that the watches, as finely calibrated as they are, will disagree. He'll then have to settle matters in one of three ways.

First, if all the watches disagree (perhaps reading 22.4, 22.5, and 22.6), the middle time is chosen. But if two watches show the same time (22.5, 22.5, and 22.6), it's the matched time that counts. Finally, if the time on one watch is lost, the average of the two remaining times to the nearest and *slowest* tenth of a second becomes the official time; for example, if the remaining times read 22.4 and 22.5, the choice will be 22.5.

As chief timer, you're responsible for training your crews. Prior to the first event, have them operate their watches several times so that they become accustomed to their use and especially to the amount of slack in the stems. Advise them to start and stop the watches with as little extraneous arm movement as possible; an arm swing, usually done for emphasis, can delay the action of the forefinger. Remind them that they must always crouch low over the edge of the pool for the best view of the swimmer's touch; they should be prepared to be splashed and must keep themselves from instinctively backing off.

And some reminders for you: On hearing the "take your mark" command, order the crews to check their watches to see that the sweep hands are properly positioned. Should there be a false start, call for the watches to be reset. At the end of the race, pass the word that the watches are not to be reset until the official times are recorded and the crews are instructed to do so.

On arriving at the pool, you should immediately obtain the watches from the meet director. They should come attached to neck cords so they can be carried without danger of being dropped into the water. Check that each watch is working properly and then prewind them all. You're responsible for collecting the watches at day's end and returning them to the meet director.

The Stroke Inspector at Work The success of your work hinges on your knowledge of correctly executed swimming strokes. To learn your trade, you'll need to study the rules surrounding each type of stroke and then watch a good many swimmers in action. In common with all meet officials, of course, you'll do your best work right from the start if you yourself are an experienced competitive swimmer.

Your work sends you along the side of the pool as you watch the lanes assigned to you. Swimming strokes are best judged from behind, but you should take pains to study them also from the side, front, and top; be careful, though, of the side view because the refraction of the water can play tricks on you. Do not call a violation unless you're absolutely certain of what you've seen. If you suspect a problem, follow the swimmer closely before reaching a decision.

By far the greatest number of stroke violations are seen in meets below college level and are most often the result of inexperience or youthful exuberance. It's highly important, then, that you religiously call every observed violation and do not "forgive" any competitor because of his youth. A forgiving attitude is a disservice. It does nothing to help the youngster overcome his faults and, if he's at all aware of what he's doing, encourages him to think that he can get away with the same thing in the future.

On sighting a violation, you must signal the referee immediately by raising one arm overhead with the palm extended. As soon as the race ends, report the violation in detail to the referee. The referee or the starter should then explain the violation to the swimmer with an eye to preventing a recurrence in the future.

The Turn Judge at Work Essentially the demands of your job match those of the stroke inspectors. Crouching at the end of your lane, you must be thoroughly acquainted with the turn and pushoff rules for each type of stroke. You must call only the violations that you actually see. You must immediately signal a violation by raising one hand overhead with the palm extended. A full report of the violation them must be made to the referee at the end of the race.

The Takeoff Judge at Work You work only the relay races. Your job is to see that each swimmer does not enter the race ahead of time. Before he leaves the starting line, the teammate ahead of him must touch the finish pad.

To judge each start, stand so that you have a good view of the waiting swimmer and the water below. Depending on your association, you may be instructed to stand at the side of the pool or just several feet away from the waiting competitor. Focus in on an area that takes in the feet and hands of the approaching swimmer. Hold your gaze there until you see the touch and the departure.

The Mechanics of Officiating: Diving Events

Officiating a diving competition is principally judging work. You'll do the best job as the diving referee or as a member of the panel of judges if you've done some diving yourself, of course. But even if you've never gone off a board, you can in time become a highly competent official by devoting yourself to a careful and thorough study of the sport. You'll need to master the rules, learn to recognize the elements of a good dive (slow motion films can be an invaluable aid), and broaden your experience by watching numerous divers at work. You should also attend officiating clinics and discuss the sport with knowledgeable friends.

The Diving Referee at Work You are in charge of the competition, and your work begins as soon as you arrive at the pool. You should immediately meet with the panel of judges to discuss their coming duties, alert them to any rule changes that are in effect, and answer whatever questions they may have. They're to receive their scorecards at this time; the cards, showing the numerical values awarded for each dive, are flashed throughout the competition. They often come in a flip-type scorebook for easy handling.

Another early order of business is the placement of the judges at poolside. You should position them so that they have an unobstructed view of both the board and the water and can see the divers in profile. If outdoors, set them with the sun at their backs; indoors or outdoors, make sure they're not troubled by reflections off the water. If the board is centered on the pool width, the judges can be divided between the two sides of the pool. They can all work on one side of the pool if the board is well off center.

Once you've cared for the judges, your attention turns to the scoresheets. These are the lists of dives submitted by the competitors. You (or another authorized official if you're pressed for time) must check to see that each list is correct in all its details. If an error escapes notice—perhaps the inclusion of a dive that is not permitted—the diver may lose points during the competition or even be disqualified. To avoid a loss of points, the competitor must perform the dives exactly as they're described on his scoresheet.

In any meet, a contestant must perform a combination of required and optional dives, with the actual number being determined by the rules of the sponsoring association. NFSHSA rules, for example, call for five required dives and six optionals—all chosen from specified groups of dives—in championship meets. At other meets, one required dive and five optionals are contested.

The dives are divided among preliminary, semifinal, and final rounds (in a championship meet, for instance, the eleven dives can be broken down into two requireds and three optionals for the preliminaries, two requireds and one optional for the semifinals, and one required and two optionals in the finals). Divers with the lowest scores are eliminated as the competition progresses. A diver's standing in the final order of finish is determined by his cumulative score for all the rounds. If two or more divers end with the same number of points, they're declared tied. No additional dives are staged to break the tie.

Once the competition begins, your primary job is to help the judges score the dives in accordance with the rules. In the main, you watch for performance flaws that require specific adjustments in the number of points to be awarded. Specifically, you:

- Look for violations in the diver's forward approach. The forward approach must be straight and smooth, of not less than three steps, and must be followed by a jump off one foot to a landing on both feet at the end of the board. If there's a violation somewhere along the line, you're to deduct two points from the score awarded by each judge.
- Watch for balks—the diver's failure to complete the approach, the takeoff, or the dive. Again, you must deduct two points from the scores awarded. Two balks can see the diver disqualified.
- Judge when a dive is "unsatisfactory" or "failed" and instruct the judges as to the maximum number of points that now may be awarded under the rules. Dives can be judged unsatisfactory or failed on a number of counts, with the NFSHSA listing fourteen causes for the failed dive alone. One reason for an unsatisfactory judgment: the dive is performed in a position other than the one described on the competitor's scoresheet. And one reason for a failed effort: the diver twists his shoulders ninety degrees more or less than is indicated on his scoresheet.

In addition to watching the dives, you sound your whistle when each ends. There's a five-second wait, and then you request the judges to show the values they've given the effort. You're to read off the scores so that the scorer can post them; at a championship meet, you may be assisted by a *secretary of diving* who posts the scores and then delivers them to the scorer. At the close of the competition, you check the scorer's tabulations and, if everything is in order, sign the scoresheets. Once the meet referee adds his signature to the sheets, the score becomes official and cannot be changed.

The Diving Judges at Work Scoring is done along a scale running from a maximum of ten to zero, with the points descending in half-point steps. Further, the performance of each dive is judged on a quality scale graduated downward from "very good" to "failed." By formula, certain point ranges are assigned to each quality. The formulas differ among the associations. The following one comes from the NFSHSA:

1. Very good: 8.5–10
2. Good: 6.5–8
3. Satisfactory: 5–6
4. Deficient: 2.5–4.5
5. Unsatisfactory: .5–2
6. Failed: O

When there are three judges on the panel, the values shown on their scorecards after each dive are totaled. The competitor's score for his effort is then found by multiplying that total with the "degree of difficulty" factor assigned to the dive (the NFSHSA, for instance, awards a 2.0 factor for a one-meter forward somersault in the tuck position, and a 2.2 in the pike). When there are more than three judges on hand, the top and bottom values are usually eliminated so that only the middle three remain for the computation.

It goes without saying that you must be intimately acquainted with the rules that encompass the various dives. And you must have a firm understanding of the *ideal* manner in which each dive can be executed. On this latter point, the following suggestions should be of particular help in your first meets:

• Remember that in addition to being smooth and straight, the approach should be graceful, without stiff arms and exaggerated toe-pointing. Do not, however, penalize individual mannerisms.
• The takeoff should be strong. Check the diver's angle of lean and the coordination of his arms and legs as he depresses the board and then springs away. On the jump at the end of the approach, it's proper for the diver to point his toes and bring his leg up until his thigh is about parallel with the board. On the standing takeoff, he may move the board up and down several times, but he may not leave it before his final spring and takeoff.
• Watch the diver's elevation as he leaves the board. It should be high enough to permit him to execute the dive properly, but not so high that it will damage the precision of the dive. While good elevation is always desirable, a lack of it is not to be considered bad, particularly in small competitors, if it doesn't harm the execution of the dive.
• Concentrate on how gracefully and precisely the dive is executed. The diver should be in full control of his body throughout the effort. If the

tuck or pike position is in play, it should be tight, with the toes well pointed.
- The entry should be clean and vertical, with the toes pointed. One caution, however: because it's the last thing you see, the entry can influence your judgment too much unless you're careful. You'll find it easy to give a poor dive a higher score than it deserves if the entry happens to be a good one. *So always be sure to judge the entire dive.*

Like the officials in all sports, you must strive for consistency in your judgments. If one performance earns a value of 6.5 on your scorecard, be sure that subsequent performances of a similar quality are given the same score. Above all, don't let your personal feelings about a diver influence your calls. Assign your value for the dive and not the diver. Treat all divers, regardless of their skills, in exactly the same manner throughout the competition.

Finally, always score *downard* rather than upward. Instead of starting with zero and proceeding from there, begin with ten in mind. Envision the dive as it would look when perfectly executed. Compare the actual dive with the imagined effort, seeing how closely the two match. Then pick the appropriate value.

Your Uniform

There is no specified uniform for swimming officials. But the NFSHSA suggests that all the officials dress similarly, stipulating that the attire always be clean and unwrinkled. White clothing and shoes are felt to be very acceptable attire.

10. In Alphabetical Order

THERE ARE A NUMBER of sports that, while popular, are not as widely played as the games covered in the preceding chapters. Some, such as lacrosse, are traditionally limited to particular geographical areas. One—ice hockey—demands snapping cold weather, though climate as a factor is now diminishing with the spread of indoor rinks across the country. Another—water polo—appeals to accomplished swimmers only.

Though individually not as popular as the likes of football and basketball, together they still attract thousands of young competitors. Their need for competent officials is as great as that in any other sport. In this chapter we're going to look at the officiating basics for seven of these sports. As the chapter title indicates, we'll take the seven in alphabetical order.

Badminton

Badminton is officiated in much the same manner as tennis, and the game itself, though it uses a shuttle rather than a ball, is quite similar to tennis. Once you've read this section, you will find it helpful to check Chapter Six. It contains a number of suggestions that you can put to use.

204

At maximum, badminton is officiated by a crew of twelve. The officials are the *umpire,* the *service judge,* and ten *linesmen.* In a pinch, a match can be adequately handled without the service judge and by as few as four (or even two) linesmen.

Like tennis, badminton is customarily played in tournaments. The tournament is usually served by a referee. He is charged with seeing that the day progresses smoothly and that the games are played in accordance with the rules. Unless the crew is shorthanded, he does not actually officiate any of the matches.

When working as umpire, you view the game from a platform located just off center court that places you above the net. You're in complete charge of the match, supervising the linesmen and acknowledging their calls and keeping score. If there's a service judge working the match, he'll watch the server on each service while you keep an eye on the receivers.

There will be times when a tournament, especially a small one, will be without a referee. You'll then be the final authority on all disputed matters in the match. If there is a referee, points under debate should be referred to him for settlement.

Your work begins before the match when you check the net height and assign the linesmen to their positions. Basically, each linesman is to call shuttles coming into his area that are out of bounds or strike the ground before being hit. The linesmen are to be stationed as illustrated. The circled positions are those that can be eliminated when you're not working with a full crew. If a crew is reduced to four, the umpire is responsible for covering the short service lines; the linesmen at the corners will then be additionally responsible for the back boundary line.

Prior to the match, you should obtain three or four properly weighted shuttles and have them ready for play. You should not, however, change shuttles during the match unless there is a good reason to do so.

Once the match begins, you must, of course, follow the action closely. Extra attention given to the following points should be of particular help in your first days. In time they and all other aspects of officiating should become second nature to you.

- On each service, if there's not a service judge with you, check that the shuttle is below the server's waist when struck. Actually, in the absence of a service judge, you'll find that the nearby linesmen are better positioned to judge the legality of the serving stroke. Assign a linesman to

45.

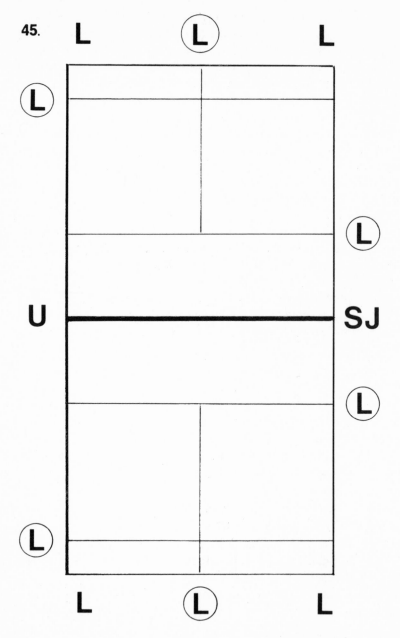

the job of watching and judging the serve with you. Also, keep an eye out for those illegal shots—the "scoop" and the "throw."

- Again on the service, check that no player on the "out" side (the receiver's) moves out of his court before the shuttle is delivered.
- At all times in the match keep your eyes on the shuttle. Judge where it is to arrive and focus on that spot an instant ahead of time so you'll have a clear view of the action there.
- Watch for the player who strikes the shuttle before it passes the net and for the player who touches the net or its supports with his clothing, his racket, or any part of his body before the shuttle is dead. Both are infractions that bring a loss of point.
- Make certain that the players change sides at the proper score in the third game.
- When the game comes to a score at which setting is permitted, don't forget to ask the player who first reached the score if he wishes to set.
- At times, you'll not be able to make a decision because the action involved was not clearly seen. You'll need to turn to the players for advice. They're honor-bound to give you an honest opinion. That opinion should be accepted if all the players agree to it. Otherwise, overlook the suspected problem and call a "let" to restart the action.

Some general points of officiating are the same as in tennis. Make your calls promptly, but do not call any infraction unless it's actually seen. Never anticipate an infraction and run the risk of calling it prematurely; wait until you see it. Your various decisions and the score at the end of each rally need to be announced aloud; speak in a clear and strong voice so that you can be easily heard by the players and the spectators. At the end of the match, check your scorecard closely before signing it. The card should then be filed with the proper meet authority.

Boxing

Each association and state has its own regulations governing the conduct and officiating of a boxing match. What follows here is a discussion of general officiating procedures that, with their accent on the safety of the competitors, are universally accepted.

Ideally, six officials should be on hand for each bout on the card—a *referee,* at least two *judges,* a *timer,* a *counter,* and a *physician.*

The referee is in complete charge of the match and supervises its conduct. The judges award the points that decide the winner; if there are only two judges, the referee also serves as a judge. The timer not only times the rounds but also the knockdowns and the between-round intermissions. The counter, who works only when there is a knockdown, takes the count from the timer and signals it to the ring so that the referee can pick it up; the procedure frees the timer from signaling and allows him to concentrate fully on the clock. Virtually all states require that a doctor be on the premises at all times to advise on the physical condition of the boxers and determine whether a competitor is able to continue the bout.

Your sponsoring association also has the right to have a representative on hand to see that the officiating crew is following the procedures necessary for the protection of the competitors. He has the authority to dismiss any official on the spot—the referee especially—not found to be working up to standard.

Should you referee a match, your work will begin far in advance of the opening bell. On arriving at the arena, you're to:

- Examine the ring. In particular, check that there are the correct number of ropes (three) along each side and that they're adjusted to the proper tension. The mat also must be checked to see that it's clear of foreign substances. The thickness of the mat must be up to regulation.
- Meet with the crew. Ascertain that each man knows his job. Of greatest importance, check with the doctor as to exactly where he'll be seated at ringside. Urge him not to leave his place during the match. You must know where he is at all times.
- Check each fighter's equipment. Each boxer must be outfitted with trunks, appropriate shoes, cup, mouthpiece, and jersey. No competitor may wear any personal item (religious medal, good-luck charm, etc.) that poses a danger to himself or his opponent.
- Check the boxers' gloves and bandages to be sure that the gloves are the correct weight for the age classification (glove weights run from six to fourteen ounces) and that the thickness and weight of the bandages and tape are up to regulation.
- Meet with the fighters to give them their prebout instructions. This meeting is usually held at the weigh-in some minutes before the first event. At the same time, talk with the seconds so that they understand the behavior that you consider appropriate at ringside.

You should be uniformed and ready for your prebout duties at least forty-five minutes before the first match. Your uniform consists of slacks, a shirt of a given color (usually determined by your sponsoring association), and athletic shoes. The uniform at all times should be clean and well pressed.

On entering the ring, check it once again to make certain that everything continues to be up to standard. Likewise, as the boxers stand in their corners, give their equipment and gloves another check. In particular, take a look at the glove lacings. The laces must be securely taped down so that their ends won't fly into the opponent's face. Finally, each fighter's face is not to be greased or oiled in any way.

After the competitors have been introduced (a job that you may have to do yourself if there is not a ring announcer on hand), call them to the center of the ring for their final instructions. What is said at this point is pretty traditional. The following example can be used as a model:

"The rules have already been explained to you. Do you have any questions?" (Pause for their response.) "In case of a knockdown, I want you to go to the farthest corner and stay there until I direct you to continue. A mandatory eight-count is in effect. You can take it on your feet. You're to protect yourself at all times and come out fighting at the bell. Shake hands now and not again until the end of the bout."

Now for your supervision of the match itself. Four basic points should always be at the front of your mind:

- Your principal responsibility is the protection of the boxers. You can protect them only if you're on the move at all times, positioning yourself so that you can see the blows being struck by both youngsters. Your best spot is to their sides and midway between them. And the best view of their gloves and hits is to be had by focusing on the gap between them. Move in close but not close enough to interfere. Never— but *never*—take a stationary position in a corner and try to view the fight from there.
- Ideally, you should never be forced to touch the boxers. When giving them their prebout instructions at the weigh-in, stress that you want them to respond instantly to your voice commands, especially the "break" order. If a competitor refuses to disentangle himself on your command, you have no choice but to step into the middle of things,

move the offender back with the words, "Break and step back," and warn him to pay better attention. If a competitor persists in ignoring you, he can lose points or be disqualified.

- While watching the boxers, you should also keep an eye on their seconds. The seconds must not administer any aid or substance during a round (seconds have been known to wave smelling salts in a boxer's face after he's been knocked into his own corner). Nor may the seconds coach from the corner. On this point, you have to use your own judgment as to what constitutes "coaching." There's bound to be the yelling—"Keep your guard up ... use your left"—that's traditional at ringside. It can pretty well be ignored, but only if it doesn't interfere with the bout.

- You must constantly be alert to each boxer's physical condition. Keep asking and answering one question: is he being hurt so that he can't defend himself or is he in danger of an injury that can damage him permanently? If you even slightly suspect a "yes" answer in either case, *do not wait until the end of the round before having the youngster checked.* Call time immediately and summon the doctor; have him check the competitor and let him be the one who determines whether the fight should continue or not. Never make any sort of medical decision on your own.

- If you sense that a boxer is only slightly injured, you may wait until between rounds to check or have him checked. But be very sure of yourself before you take this route.

- You should also stop the bout immediately if you see that a youngster is hopelessly outclassed and in danger of being injured. Should a competitor drop his mouthpiece, call time and then make sure that it's back in place before allowing the bout to continue.

- Should there be a knockdown, don't be concerned with the nicety of getting the standing fighter to the farthest corner. Rather, go directly to the downed boxer, check his condition as you make the count, and if he seems at all hurt, immediately summon the doctor.

One type of injury is quite difficult to assess. It's easy to judge the damage if a youngster suffers, say, a cut above the eye. But what about the boxer who absorbs a great deal of punishment without showing any outward harm? He can be hurt severely if you're not especially careful. Always watch for the danger signs of hidden damage—too many solid blows by the opponent, a loss of coordination, wobbly knees, glazed eyes, and the inability to answer such simple questions as "How many fingers am I showing?" Depending on the circumstances, you might want to start by checking the youngster between rounds and asking his seconds for an honest evaluation of his condition. If you're at all nervous, summon the doctor for his opinion.

Should you be working with just two judges, you'll need to join them in scoring the rounds. Virtually all amateur bouts run for three rounds. At grade-school level, the rounds are one minute each. Junior and senior high boxers usually fight two-minute rounds. Three-minute rounds come into play in college bouts. Regardless of the level, the rounds are customarily scored by points.

A ten- or twenty-point scoring system is ordinarily used. The system calls for the winner of a round to be awarded the full number of available points—say, twenty—while the loser is given a "deserving" share, perhaps fifteen, perhaps eighteen, or whatever total seems appropriate. At the end of the bout, the competitor with the greater number of points is the winner.

Basically, points are scored for what are known as "effective blows." Today's gloves come with a white band stretching up the backs of the fingers and over the knuckles. For a blow to be effective, the opponent must be struck with the white band. The boxer who lands more effective blows in a round takes that round. By itself, the power of a punch does not count for scoring purposes. But by causing the opponent to slow down and thus enabling a great number of effective blows to be landed, it does count.

When awarding a round, however, you shouldn't limit yourself to a count of the effective blows. Other factors have to be taken into consideration. One is the fighter's aggressiveness; he must be looked on with judging favor if he takes the fight to the opponent. Second, there is what is called ring generalship. In some degree, your scoring must recognize how he controls the bout through feints and other maneuvers, how he keeps his opponent off balance, and how his boxing skill outshines the skill of the opponent.

At the end of the bout, if there's not a ring announcer present, you'll be called on to announce the judge's decisions. It's traditional to raise the winner's arm overhead in the victory signal. Both boys should be congratulated for doing their best and presenting a fine competition.

Ice Hockey

Today both amateur and professional hockey are officiated by the same number of officials, eight in all. They are the *referee,* two *linesmen,* two *goal judges,* a *timekeeper,* a *penalty timekeeper,* and a *scorekeeper.*

The referee heads the crew and is in complete charge of the game. The linesmen and goal judges assist by making certain calls for him, but all final decisions concerning the play are his. He's the only official authorized to impose a penalty that sends a player off the ice.

The linesmen, working the area around the blue lines, are responsible for calling offsides, offside passes, and icing. They also retrieve the puck when play is halted and then drop it for the face-offs in the neutral zone. In general, linesmen do not call penalties but are free to report infractions to the referee. The referee may also turn to them for their version of an infraction under question.

The goal judges are divided between the two goals. Each sits in an off-ice area (usually screened) just behind his goal. His single job is to determine whether or not the puck crosses the goal line for a score. On seeing a goal scored, he signals the referee by raising his arm or, in a well-outfitted arena, by switching on a red light in front of his area. He then reports the details of the goal to the referee, after which the referee has the final decision on whether the score was legally made.

The timekeeper operates the game clock and signals the end of each period, using a buzzer or some other audio device to do so. His companion, the penalty timekeeper, checks the time served off-ice by penalized players and keeps an accurate record of the times when the penalty periods begin and end.

The scorekeeper maintains a complete and accurate record of the game. Contained in it are notations on the goals scored, the players scoring them, the players assisting, the goalkeeper saves, the times that goals are scored, the players penalized, and the times of the penalties.

Because of its speed and its tradition of hard-charging play, hockey is anything but an easy game to officiate. But the mechanics of its officiating can be easily described. Only the referee and the linesmen, of course,

46.

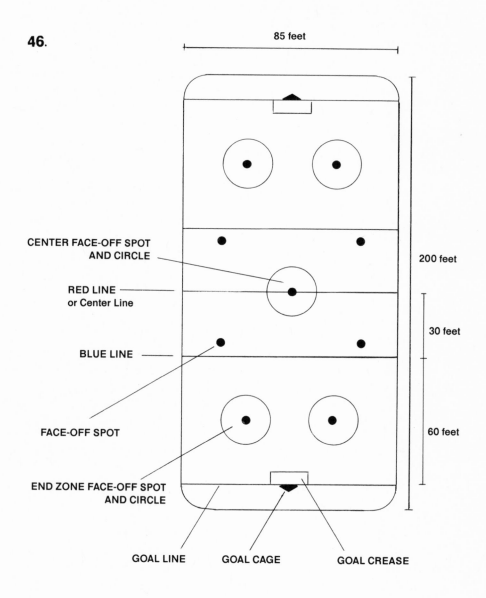

85 feet

CENTER FACE-OFF SPOT
AND CIRCLE

RED LINE
or Center Line

BLUE LINE

FACE-OFF SPOT

END ZONE FACE-OFF SPOT
AND CIRCLE

200 feet

30 feet

60 feet

GOAL LINE   GOAL CAGE   GOAL CREASE

work out on the ice. The referee tracks the action by skating the length of the rink with the players. Unlike the soccer referee, however, he does not cover the playing area on a diagonal; rather, he always skates along one sideboard. The linesmen, as mentioned earlier, limit their movements to the blue line areas.

When you're out on the ice, the followng points should be kept firmly in mind:

- The welfare of the players must always be a basic concern. Such dangerous maneuvers as board checking, cross checking, and slashing must be instantly and strictly penalized. And they must be penalized right from the start of the game. Don't ease into the action and be lenient in the opening minutes. Leniency here can open the door to an epidemic of rough play.
- In keeping with the above point, watch closely when the players are battling it out in front of a goal. Sound your whistle as soon as the puck disappears from view. Fast action here protects the goalkeeper and prevents the piling on and in-fighting that can so easily result in injury.
- Whenever sounding your whistle, give it a hard blast so that the players are certain to hear you. Several blasts are usually in order.
- As you know, the basic purpose of a penalty is to keep a team from gaining an illegal advantage over its opponent. This point must be remembered in your timing on the whistle. The whistle itself must not add to the disadvantage. For instance, you should not whistle immediately if, on seeing that an offensive player is offside in his attacking zone, you sense that the defensive unit has a good chance to make an offensive thrust out of the zone; wait until you see how the play turns out. Conversely, you should hit the whistle immediately on other offensive infractions so that the team cannot further capitalize on its drive.

As a hockey official, you'll need to develop the ability to skate backwards. Back-pedaling is a must when the players are coming out of their defensive zones. They should always be kept to your front. Don't turn away until they're clear of the zone.

Lacrosse

Often called "the fastest game on two feet," lacrosse is officiated by a four-man crew—a *referee,* and *assistant referee,* a *timekeeper,* and a *score-keeper.*

The timing and scorekeeping duties are pretty much the same as in other sports; additionally, substitutes must always report to the score-keeper and are not to enter the field until he releases them. The referee and assistant referee—customarily dressed in black-and-white vertically striped shirts, white knickers, and dark hose—work much as do their counterparts in basketball and soccer. The following illustrations prove the point.

The face-off starts each period and restarts the action after a goal. Taken at the center circle, it's supervised by the official (Official 1 above) who is working the side of the field opposite the timing and scoring table. He places the ball in the circle, checks the positions of the opposing cen-

47.

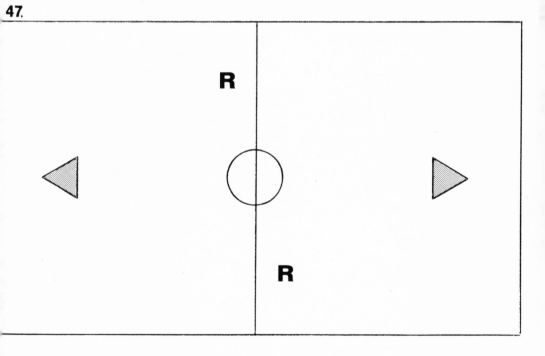

ters' crosses (sticks), backs out of the circle, and launches the play with his whistle. The free official, stationed across the field on a narrow diagonal from the supervising official, watches the surrounding players for fouls and violations. He's especially on the alert for players who may illegally enter the circle.

Once the ball is in play, the officials divide the field diagonally between themselves as in two-official soccer. Each man is primarily responsible for the action in his area. He is free, however, to call infractions that he sights over in his companion's area and—in the interests of cooperation and full coverage—should always do so.

As in basketball and soccer, the officials employ the lead-trail system. One man leads the play, arriving at last at a point to the side and behind the goal when the ball closes in on that target. His partner follows the play. In this way they have the action surrounded—from either side and fore-and-aft. They exchange jobs when the players turn and sweep up-

48.

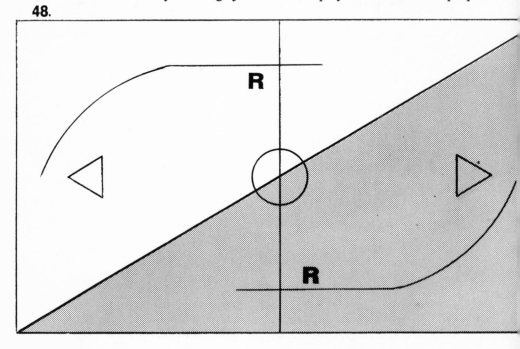

field. (Please see Chapters Four and Five for further details on the lead-trail system.)

When the action is around the goal, the lead official should concentrate on the player with the ball and on all goal shots. The trail man is responsible for covering the general play. He should be especially alert for interference infractions and for players entering the crease.

As fast and as heated as its action is, lacrosse needs the wide variety of infractions listed in its rulebooks. They range from illegal substitutions and interference to holding, tripping, pushing, and illegally slashing. Fouls customarily involve a loss of playing time for the offender. A one-minute loss is the usual penalty for accidental fouls. Two- and three-minute penalties are called for deliberate or flagrant infractions. A foul intended to injure another player—perhaps by kneeing, kicking, or striking him with a stick—gets the offender expelled from the game. Expulsion must also be imposed if a player throws down his stick and swings at an opponent, no matter what the provocation. If the opponent brought on the attack by a foul or unnecessarily rough play, he, too, should be penalized.

Fouls are called much in the manner of basketball. On sighting trouble, sound your whistle sharply. Point to the offending player and name him aloud by number. Then, clearly and in a strong voice, announce the foul and the length of the penalty being imposed. At the same time, signal the infraction to the timing and scoring table. If the offending player gives you an argument, you may assess him an additional minute of penalty time.

Because lacrosse can be quite as rough as hockey, your principal officiating concern must be the safety of the players. Call infractions immediately (except in those instances when the whistle must be delayed until the action ends). Call them consistently, not being lenient at one moment and strict at another. Call them right from the moment the game opens; no easing into the action, please. Always sound the whistle sharply.

Prior to the game the referee and assistant referee are to check the field, the goal and its net, and the players' crosses and equipment to see that everything is up to standard and in proper working order. Special attention should be given to the crosse heads; they should be firmly laced so that the lacings will not come loose during play and hinder the action or pose a danger to the players. At game's end the referee must check and sign the scoresheet.

Softball

The playing rules of baseball and softball are, with a few minor exceptions, the same. So are the techniques of officiating. A full account of your duties and calls, then, can be had by reading Chapter Two. In this section, we'll look only at the differences between the two games.

The first difference is seen in the dimensions of the fields. The baselines in baseball measure ninety feet, and the mound-to-plate distance is sixty feet six inches, though both these dimensions can be reduced (as they are in Little League) for younger players. In softball the baselines run sixty feet each, with the mound-to-plate distance determined by whether the game is played by men or women. The customary delivery distance in both fast and slow pitch is forty-six feet for men. For women, it's forty feet in fast pitch and forty-six feet in slow pitch. Of course, all softball field dimensions can be reduced for younger players.

So far as play itself is concerned, there are only two major differences between the games. The first concerns the pitcher while the second has to do with the baserunners.

Pitching In baseball the pitcher is allowed to deliver from either a windup or set position, with the latter being used to hold runners close to their bases before the pitch. The softball pitcher, however, is limited to one style of delivery.

He must start the delivery with both feet touching the pitcher's plate and come to a full stop for at least two seconds before throwing. Then he must step towards the batter, execute no more than one windmill motion, and end with the throw delivered underhand. The wrist must be brought below hip level and must be no further out from the body than the elbow.

As in baseball, any violation of the rules governing a proper delivery results in an illegal pitch. The penalties for an illegal pitch, which is called a balk when there are runners on base, are the same in both games. When the bases are empty, the pitch is judged a "ball," and the ball is declared dead. A balk advances the runners a base; the ball is declared dead, but a "ball" is not called on the batter.

The penalties, however, are not to be enforced if the illegal pitch causes the batter to advance at least one base or enables the runners to advance at least a base. For this reason, though you should immediately call "illegal pitch" or "ball" on seeing an infraction, you should hold back on any further decision until the subsequent action indicates whether a ruling will be necessary.

Baserunners Baserunners in baseball are allowed to leave a base—lead off—before the pitch. Not so in softball. The runner must remain in contact with his base until the pitch is released. If he steps off ahead of time, you must call him out.

The runner in softball is also to be judged out if, following a pitch or a play, he fails to return to his base or advance to the next one by the time the ball is returned to within an eight-foot radius of the pitcher's plate.

These two technicalities, especially the latter one, can cause you some headachy close calls. You'll need those two sets of eyes that your colleagues in baseball find so helpful—one for the ball and one for the runner's feet.

Umpire Positioning As in amateur baseball, two umpires can handle a softball game—the plate umpire and the field umpire. The duties of the plate umpire are identical in both games. But when serving as the field umpire, you'll need to choose starting positions that are somewhat different than those used in baseball. Shown in the illustration are the recommended starting positions when: the bases are empty (Point A); a runner is on first (Point B); a runner is on second, runners are at first and second, or the bases are loaded (Point C) and; a runner is at third or runners are at first and second (Point D). If you wish, you may station yourself at Point E when a runner is at third.

Water Polo

Two *referees,* two *goal judges,* three *timekeepers,* and a *scorekeeper* are the officials needed for a water polo match. As a member of the crew, you'll find that the game in several of its details is similar to soccer.

49.

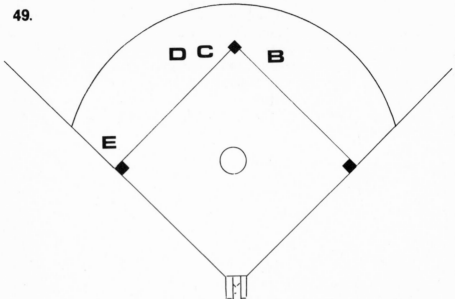

The referees, working along the deck to either side of the pool, control the conduct of the game and make all decisions on the play. The goal judges, who are ordinarily used only during championship competitions, signal when goals are scored and assist in the supervision of certain of the free throws that follow infractions.

Each timekeeper is charged with an individual set of responsibilities. One records the periods of actual play, records time-outs and intermissions, operates the game clock, and posts the score on the scoreboard. Another operates the thirty-five-second clock and notifies the referees of violations of the thirty-five-second rule (the rule states that a team on gaining possession of the ball must shoot at the opponent's goal within thirty-five seconds; failure to do so sends the ball to the opposition). The third keeps track of players whose infractions get them ejected from the game for specified lengths of time; he signals when the penalized players may re-enter the water.

The scorer keeps a complete record of the game. In addition, he informs the referees when a team has used its maximum number of time-outs (three for the first four quarters and one in overtime) and when a player has posted his third personal foul.

The mechanics of officiating call for the referees to divide the action between themselves. One handles all the forecourt play at both ends of the pool. The other covers the backcourt action at both ends of the pool. Should you work the forecourt, you'll be the game's senior official. You'll be the final authority on all disputed points.

If you're assigned to the backcourt, you must be prepared to take on several additional jobs. You'll be called on to (1) observe that all ejected players re-enter the playing area in the appropriate manner, slipping rather than diving into the water, (2) watch that substitutions are properly made and at the correct times, and (3) signal the restart of play with a whistle after a goal has been scored. You must also keep an eye on the game and thirty-five-second clocks to see that they're being operated efficiently. Should you glimpse an error on either clock, you're to have it corrected immediately.

50.

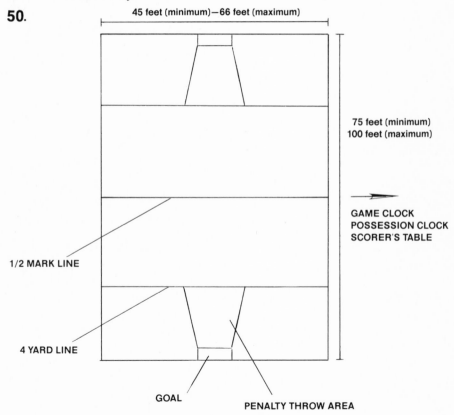

45 feet (minimum)—66 feet (maximum)

75 feet (minimum)
100 feet (maximum)

GAME CLOCK
POSSESSION CLOCK
SCORER'S TABLE

1/2 MARK LINE

4 YARD LINE

GOAL

PENALTY THROW AREA

51. WATER POLO SIGNALS

Penalty Throw

Offensive
Dead Time Faults
(Hold 5 Seconds)

Technical
Ordinary Fouls
Goal Throw
Corner Throw

Face-off

Goal

From *Water Polo Rulebook*, The National Federation of State High School Assn's

As referees, you and your partner control the game with visual and audio signals. Working out of the water as you do, you're more removed from the players than are the officials in most other sports. Always sound your whistle sharply and make your signals decisively and distinctly so that there's no chance of a player missing or misinterpreting them. To help you, the home team is required to equip you with one of the most unusual signaling devices in officiating—the "double flag."

The flag consists of a thirty-six-inch staff with a twelve-inch square banner at each end. The banners—one often colored dark blue or black and the other white—each stand for a team. Basically, the flag is used to flash four signals. Each is flashed in its own way. Here's how you should handle things in each instance.

• When signaling a free throw, sound your whistle and immediately display the banner of the team being awarded the throw, keeping the other banner bunched in your hand. Extend the flag diagonally towards the water. With your free hand, point to the spot where the throw is to be taken. Hold the pose until you're sure that all players have seen it.

There are three kinds of free throw. Each is awarded in the wake of a technical or ordinary foul. Two—the corner and goal throws—are used to put the ball back in play after it has been sent out of bounds (a technical foul) and are the twins of the corner and goal kicks in soccer. The remaining free throw follows ordinary fouls and all other technicals. The National Federation of State High School Associations (NFSHSA) lists seventeen technicals and three categories of "ordinaries" in its rulebook. An example of a technical: violating the thirty-five-second rule. An ordinary: illegally interfering with an opponent.

• When signaling a penalty throw, once again sound the whistle sharply, but this time raise the flag directly overhead with the banner of the team to make the throw displayed. Hold up your free hand and extend four fingers. The four fingers are the key to indicating the throw; it must be made at the four-yard marker. Again, hold the pose until it's seen by everyone.

The penalty throw is the equivalent of the penalty kick in soccer. It is awarded for a variety of offenses—the NFSHSA lists nine general categories. Example: An offensive player while in control of the ball and facing the goal, is fouled within the penalty zone by being shoved, pulled back, or pushed under the water.

• When signaling a face-off, hold the flag horizontally in front of your midsection, allowing both banners to dangle. With your free hand, point to the spot where the face-off will be played.

The face-off is used to restart the action in a variety of circumstances. For instance, it's your only choice for retriggering things when both teams have fouled simultaneously and you're unable to decide which infraction came first. Two opponents then face each other. You throw the ball into the water, making certain to target it so that the two men have an equal opportunity to reach it.

• When signaling a goal, again hold the flag at its midpoint so that each banner is displayed. Raise it straight overhead.

The flag is also used to signal the ejection of a player. On an ejection, point the flag at the offending player simultaneously calling his cap color and number to the players in the water. Repeat the call to the timing and scoring table so that it can be picked up there. As soon as the player begins to leave the water, raise the flag as a signal for play to restart.

Players are ejected from the game for what are called personal or major fouls. They range from deliberately splashing water in an opponent's face to an attack on a player. The NFSHSA rules list nineteen personal and major fouls. Ejection time ranges from thirty seconds to the remainder of the game.

You need to learn one last signal. When a foul occurs while the ball is dead, sound your whistle, place your hand flat on top of your head, and call out the number and cap color of the offending player. Then flash the appropriate signal for restarting the action.

The various fouls in water polo are there not only to insure a smoothly played match but to protect the players as well. The game can be dangerously rough if not strongly controlled by the officiating crew, and so you'll need to be well acquainted with the fouls and constantly on the lookout for them. Because of the action of the water, they can be difficult to see at times. Especially difficult to sight are fouling actions under the water.

Let your guides be those used by officials in all sports. Call fouls as soon as you see them, except in those instances when the whistle may put the offended team at a further disadvantage; hold the whistle, then, until the play completes itself. Treat fouls strictly from the start of the game; always remember that the leniency or the laxness that comes when you ease yourself into the opening action can open the way to trouble later on. And treat fouls with consistency throughout, not being lenient in one instance and severe in the next.

As a referee, you may wear a black-and-white striped shirt, plain-colored slacks, and athletic footwear. The NFSHSA calls for its referees to wear a white shirt or jacket, white trousers, and white footwear.

Wrestling

The number of officials assigned to a wrestling crew hinges on the type of meet being held. A *referee,* a *timekeeper,* and a *scorekeeper* are needed for dual meets. A championship meet should see them joined by several *mat judges.* In addition, the National Federation of State High School Associations (NFSHSA) recently approved the use of an *assistant referee.*

The referee, uniformed in a black-and-white striped knit shirt and dark slacks and shoes, supervises the match and exercises complete control over it. The timer is not only responsible for keeping time on the match (matches usually run for six minutes and are divided into three periods of two minutes each) but also for recording the accumulated time-outs taken for official conferences or injuries. The scorer records the points awarded the wrestlers by the referee as the match progresses; the referee signals the points from the mat.

The mat judges are on hand to assist the referee in his calls, as is the assistant referee. The judges who kneel or sit off the mat, are permitted to disagree with the referee's calls; in the event of a disagreement, the judges signal the referee; he stops the action and consults with them to settle the matter. The judges may not enter the wrestling area except to stop an evolving dangerous situation that the referee may have overlooked.

The assistant referee works in the wrestling area with the referee and provides the match with extra coverage. The assistant makes calls and is free to disagree with any call by the referee. But the referee is still completely in charge of the match, and if there is a disagreement, his decision will prevail.

Though mat judges and the assistant referee are needed principally at championships, there is nothing to stop them from participating in dual meets.

When you agree to referee a meet, you should count on arriving at least an hour in advance of the first match. The time will be needed to complete a string of premeet jobs. You're to:

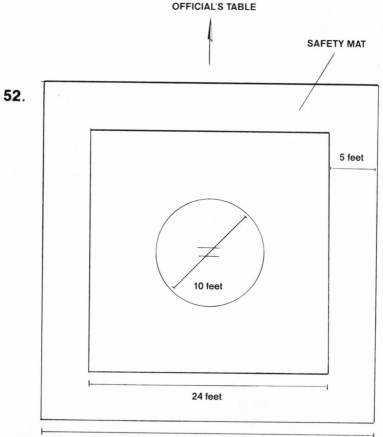

52.

OFFICIAL'S TABLE

SAFETY MAT

5 feet

10 feet

24 feet

34 feet

- Check the wrestling area, its pads, and its markings to see that everything is up to regulation and in suitable condition for the competition.
- Confer with the team coaches and competitors to clarify your interpretations of the rules and answer any questions that they may have.
- Check the wrestlers and their gear. Their uniforms must be neat and according to regulation. You must take special care to check that nothing on the uniform or the wrestler's person constitutes a danger to himself or his opponent. Fingernails, for instance, must be trimmed and smooth. If there are belt buckles with rough edges or areas, they must be taped over. Shoes should have eyelets and not hooks for the lacings.
- Supervise the weigh-in making certain that each competitor meets the required weight for his classification. If he fails to make the classification, he may enter the next highest class.
- Meet with the timekeeper and scorekeeper for a review of their duties.

With your premeet duties out of the way, you can head for the wrestling area. Here, prior to each bout, you're to call the competitors to center of the mat. Have them shake hands and give them two instructions. Tell them, first, that they're to do most of their wrestling near the mat's center circle, and second, that they're not to stop wrestling until they hear your whistle.

Matches begin from a standing start. Each competitor then seeks an advantageous position that will enable him to take his opponent down to the mat. Position the wrestlers so that they're facing each other across the center circle. Your own position is at the edge of the circle and facing the scoring table. When you see that everything is in readiness, sound your whistle.

Subsequent periods open with what is called the referee's position. The position calls for the competitors to kneel in the center circle at right angles to each other with one competitor's head above the other's back. The position is also used to restart the match after the wrestlers have gone off the mat while one wrestler held the advantage and after the match has been stopped because of injury, again while one man held the advantage.

When starting the wrestlers from the referee's position, crouch down at the edge of the circle and make sure that it is being properly taken. Then raise your hand to signal that you're about to launch the action. A blast on your whistle accompanied by a downward sweep of your hand starts things.

The art of refereeing a wrestling match is a complex one. You'll need to be intimately acquainted with all the rules, with all the holds that are illegal, and with all those considered potentially dangerous. A thorough study of the sport is necessary and should be complemented by watching films of wrestling bouts, learning all you can from knowledgeable fellow officials, and—above all—attending officiating clinics. The following points are intended to help you in your first days:

- When the wrestlers are on their feet at the start of the match, stay constantly on the move, traveling with them so that you always have a good view of them from the side. Maintain a little distance, though; it will keep you from interfering with their movements and will afford you the best overall view of both contestants and the limits of the mat.
- If ever you're tempted to stand still, always remember that you're in danger of having the wrestlers turn and screen some action from your view. It's an open invitation for someone to try an illegal tactic.
- While the wrestlers are still up and moving, watch in particular for stalling tactics and for an intentional backing off the mat. The match stops if the competitors leave the mat, and so the latter maneuver is often used by a youngster to keep an especially strong opponent from getting behind him and taking him down to the mat. Stalling does nothing but slow the match. Both tactics should be immediately called and penalized.
- Once the wrestlers are down on the mat, get into whatever position affords you the best view of the action. Always remember that the wrestlers can change positions with lightning speed. So watch the action closely and be prepared for sudden changes. If you miss any shifts or fail to adjust, you can cost one youngster or the other precious points.
- Watch for movements and flurries that carry the wrestlers to the edge of the mat and threaten to take them out of the wrestling area. Your best bet here is to get between the competitors and the mat edge. Warn them to stay on the mat and work towards the center.

Your prime concern must always be the safety of the wrestlers. Watch for all signs of unnecessary roughness—hitting, elbowing, kicking, lifting an opponent and throwing him down—and penalize them immediately and strictly. When the wrestlers are maneuvering for holds and counters, keep a sharp eye out for illegal holds (example: strangle holds and twisting knee lock); if you see one developing, immediately warn the man responsible; fast action here can stop the hold before it really gets started. The same goes for potentially dangerous holds (examples: double wristlock and chicken wing).

As you watch the wrestlers, you must continually signal the points being won by each. To signal, point to the competitor with one hand and raise the other, extending the appropriate number of fingers. At the same time, call out his name and the number of points. The call and the hand signal not only pass the information on to the scoring table but keep the wrestlers apprised of how the match is developing.

Points are awarded in four categories. A *takedown* earns the wrestler two points. An *escape* to a neutral position from a hold nets him one point. If he manages a *reversal* on a hold, he's given two points. A *near fall* brings him either two or three points. A fall itself ends the match.

The wrestler may also lose points for infractions. Usually one point is lost on each of his first two infractions. The penalty jumps to two points on the third infraction. A fourth infraction sees him disqualified.

Near falls can be difficult to judge because of the position and time requirements involved. For a two-point fall, the opponent's shoulders or scapulae must be held momentarily within four inches of the mat; it's also a two-point near fall when one shoulder or scapula is held momentarily against the mat while the other shoulder is held at an angle of forty-five degrees or less from the mat.

A three-point near fall is awarded when either of the two above positions is held continuously for five seconds. You're to count off the seconds silently. For best accuracy count the seconds as *one thousand and one, one thousand and two,* and so on.

A fall comes when any part of both shoulders or scapulae are held against the mat for two seconds. To make the call, you must drop into a position—most often, flat on the mat—that enables you to see the shoulders. On sighting them pressed against the mat, count off two seconds silently. It's permissible to run your hand along the mat to judge the mat-body contact. At the end of the count, slap the mat. The wrestlers should break immediately and rise to their feet.

Once the match is over, you have several jobs remaining. If the bout did not end in a fall, first check the scorer's table to obtain the point score; then call the competitors to the center of the mat and raise the winner's left arm overhead. If the match ends in a fall, the winner's arm, of course, is raised without bothering to check the scorer's table. In the event of a draw, stand between the two competitors and raise their arms simultaneously.

It's a good idea to have the competitors shake hands as you raise the winner's arm. As a number of officials point out, the technique promotes a sense of good sportsmanship and helps to reduce the embarrassment or disappointment that the loser might feel. Be sure always to congratulate both youngsters for a well-wrestled match.

BIBLIOGRAPHY

Amateur Basketball Association of the USA. *1980-1981 Handbook,* Colorado Springs, CO: ABAUSA, 1980

Bowers, Richard. *Track and Field Events: Fundamentals,* Columbus, OH: Charles E. Merrill, 1974

Bunn, John W. *The Art of Officiating Sports,* Englewood Cliffs, NJ: Prentice-Hall, 1968

Clegg, Richard and Thompson, William A. *Modern Sports Officiating,* Dubuque, IA: William C. Brown, 1979

Friedman, Arthur with Cohen, Joel H. *The World of Sports Statistics,* New York: Atheneum, 1978

Little League Baseball. *Little League Baseball: Official Regulations and Playing Rules,* Williamsport, PA: LLB, Inc., 1981

———. *The Umpire in Little League,* 1980

Matthews, Dave, McGuire, Ben, and Peterson, Jim. *Officials Manual: Soccer,* Champaign, IL: Stripes Publishing, 1972

Meyers, Carlton and Sanford, William H. *Swimming and Diving Officiating,* Palo Alto, CA: National Press, 1970

National Federation of State High School Associations. *Baseball Rule Book, 1981,* Kansas City, MO: NFSHSA, 1981

———. *Basketball Rule Book, 1980-81,* 1980

————. *Basketball Rules Simplified and Illustrated,* 1980
————. *Football Officials Manual, 1980–81,* 1980
————. *Football Rule Book, 1980,* 1980
————. *Swimming and Diving, Water Polo Rule Books, 1980–81,* 1980
————. *Track and Field Officials Manual, 1980 and 1981,* 1980
————. *Track and Field Rule Book, 1981,* 1981
————. *Volleyball Rule Book, 1980–81,* 1980
————. *Wrestling Rule Book, 1980–81,* 1980
Richards, Jack and Hill, Danny. *Complete Handbook of Sports Scoring and Record Keeping,* West Nyack, NY: Parker, 1974
United States Tennis Association. *A Friend at Court: USTA Umpires' Handbook,* Princeton: USTA; published by H. O. Zimman, Lynn, Mass, 1980
United States Volleyball Association. *The 1981 Annual Official Volleyball Reference Guide of the United States Volleyball Association,* Colorado Springs, CO: USVA, 1980
White, Jesse R. *Sports Rules Encyclopedia,* Palo Alto, CA: National Press, 1960

Edward F. Dolan, Jr., author of more than forty-five books for adults and young people, had his first book (a biography of scientist Louis Pasteur) published in 1958. His other sports books include *Starting Soccer, The Complete Beginner's Guide to Gymnastics,* and *Basic Football Strategy*. He lives with his wife, Rose, in northern California.

Calling the Play is much more than an instructional manual for the beginner. There are an estimated 150,000 men and women across the country involved in amateur officiating. Many people who love sports but choose not to participate as players have joined the growing numbers of officials at the amateur level. And many more are needed. *Calling the Play* will enable these men and women to become part of the exciting world of competitive play and give them an intelligent and purposeful guide to work with.

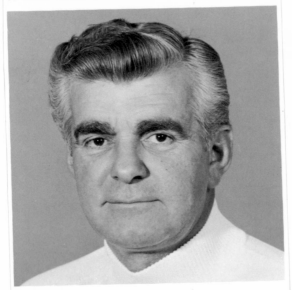

Edward F. Dolan, Jr., author of more than forty-five books for adults and young people, had his first book (a biography of scientist Louis Pasteur) published in 1958. His other sports books include *Starting Soccer, The Complete Beginner's Guide to Gymnastics*, and *Basic Football Strategy*. His lives with his wife, Rose, in northern California.